I0558308

MEMOIRS OF A ZEN MANAGER

52 WAYS TO INCREASE MANAGERIAL HAPPINESS, SUCCESS, AND EFFICIENCY

FRANCIS AUDET

Published by WSA Publishing
333 E 14th Street, #3C
New York, NY 10003

Copyright © 2024 by Francis Audet

All rights reserved. No part of this book may be reproduced or transmitted in any form or by any means, electronic or mechanical, including photocopying, recording, or by any information storage and retrieval system, without the written permission of the Publisher, except where permitted by law.

Manufactured in the United States of America and Canada, or in the United Kingdom and France when distributed elsewhere.

Audet, Francis
Memoirs of a Zen Manager
ISBN: 978-1-957013-90-9
eBook: 978-1-957013-91-6
LCCN: 2023911063

Cover design: Deividas Jablonskis
Copyediting: Wendie Pecharsky
Proofreading: Sue Toth
Interior design: Suba Murugan

www.FrancisAudet.com

Special thanks to

My friend Loïc Marchand for guiding me, helping me, reading, improving my thoughts, and challenging some approaches. Without you, this book would not be as complete.

My nieces Anika Audet and Erika Suys, whose mastery of English far exceeds mine. Without you, this book would not have the same quality and fluidity.

All of my teachers, from the small ant to the mighty tree, and all my human encounters. Without you, I would not be the person I am today.

"The real meditation is how you live your life."
                                                    — *Jon Kabat-Zinn*

CONTENTS

CONTENTS

CONTENTS

FOREWORD

AT 16 YEARS OF age, I realized that I was struggling and failing with my relationships and school and that I needed more structure and discipline and to learn more about myself and life first. After hearing about Shaolin, the Buddhist and Taoist philosophy, I became a Shaolin monk for almost six years to prepare myself and find purpose. Today, I am a successful businessman living in Dubai, and thanks to these teachings, I could heal my past relationships and build meaningful new ones. I know Francis through Shaolin.Online. As an open-minded and lifetime learner, he is very passionate about Zen and Taoist philosophy. This book should help you bring harmony, peace, and structure, not only to your corporate career, but also to your private and daily life. Learn to master and walk through life with ease no matter what obstacles you may face. Life doesn't get easier, you only become stronger, and behind every challenge you face and overcome awaits a stronger more fulfilling version of you — a kind and unshakeable person who leads by example and inner wisdom. May Francis and his guidebook help you on this journey to self-management and to lead others by example!

Thanh-Huy Nguyen
Co-founder of Shaolin.Online
Founder of Best Digital Future & Life Creator
Dubai

INTRODUCTION

IN TODAY'S FAST-PACED and constantly changing world, finding inner peace and balance can be a challenge, especially for those in management positions. The pressure to meet deadlines, exceed targets, and maintain healthy relationships with employees, customers, and stakeholders can take a toll on even the most seasoned managers and can often leave individuals feeling overwhelmed, stressed, and disconnected.

Memoirs of a Zen Manager is a unique guidebook that draws on the teachings of Buddhist and Taoist wisdom, Shaolin philosophy, the strategy to achieve efficient results expounded in Sun Tzu's *The Art of War*, and much more, to help managers navigate the challenges of their roles with grace, ease, and success. Divided into 52 weekly approaches and perspectives, this book provides readers with practical tools and insights to help cultivate a Zen-like mindset, build resilience, and create a harmonious work environment.

Through personal anecdotes and practical examples, readers will learn how to incorporate mindfulness, compassion, and self-awareness into their management style. They will discover how to tap into their inner wisdom and intuition, develop a deep sense of purpose, and cultivate meaningful relationships with their team members and

colleagues. They will be encouraged to develop self-awareness, empathy, and compassion, and to manage by example. They will learn to achieve more faster and with less
stress.

Whether you are a seasoned executive or a first-time
manager, *Memoirs of a Zen Manager* offers a fresh perspective on management that will transform the way you
think about your role and the impact you can have on
those around you. So, take a deep breath, open your mind,
and get ready to embark on a journey of self-discovery and
growth with this inspiring and thought-provoking book,
which will transform the way you approach management.

CHAPTER 1

SO WHAT IS A MANAGER?

Operational vs. Managerial

THIS IS A QUESTION I asked myself several years ago when I was a product line manager. Before, I had the narrow misconception that a manager needed to have staff reporting to them. This was not my case. Then I explored a broader sense of the term and arrived at the other end of the spectrum: Everybody is a manager. We manage our lives, our grocery lists, and our kids' agendas. In other words, we make managerial decisions all the time. This, however, was not a helpful realization in the context of the workspace.

I then looked at management from a job function perspective. This has led me to my definition of what a manager is, and I'll share that with you later on. My definition is based upon the following realization: If the activity or the job is binary, i.e., if it is either done or not, then it is in the operational domain. Am I writing this post? Yes. Then it is operational. To go beyond the operational domain and into the managerial domain, this binary perspective is not enough. Did I delegate this task? Yes. Is this management? Not really. It is the operational task of delegating.

To go from the operational domain to the managerial domain, we need to add non-binary dimensions. We need to add questions like, but certainly not limited to:

- What was the added value of the action?
- Was it done most efficiently, limiting the resources, time, effort, and energy spent on it?
- What was achieved beyond the obvious (new connections, new data, new partners, and allies)?
- Is there a thread to follow for feedback loops, improvements, deeper learning, and accomplishments?

To be in the managerial domain means going beyond the simple list of to-dos, and its binary done/not-done answers. It is a continuum and one can always improve, do better, faster, smarter, and more efficiently. Even better, one can make sure things get done naturally (through the evolution of circumstances, for example). This, I believe, is what brings us into the managerial domain.

This is what a manager should be doing. Not going down lists of to-dos, not delegating for the sake of delegating. Not saying, "I asked him to do it; I did my job."

The Pareto Principle

The Pareto Principle[1] of 20-80 teaches us that 20 percent of our actions bring us 80 percent of our results. Of course,

---

1 To learn more about the Pareto Principle, please visit https://resumelab.com/career-advice/pareto-principle

in a complete binary world, this is debatable. If my job is to paint chairs, and I paint four chairs per day, 20 chairs per week, 20 percent of my time accomplished 20 percent of my work. In the managerial domain, however, things get interesting.

Let's take a 40-hour workweek. Let's assume that 10 hours are spent on mandatory operational tasks (filling reports, attending this or that corporate meeting, etc.). That leaves us with 30 hours. Using the Pareto Principle, 6 of those hours (20 percent of 30) bring us 80 percent of the accomplishments. This in turn means that 24 hours are not spent on much relevant work (it may SEEM relevant, especially if we are going down a list of to-dos or want to lower the inbox, but in reality? What is the true added value of these tasks?).

Let's play the game one step further and redo the Pareto Principle for the remaining 24 hours: 20 percent of that time is spent doing the 80 percent more efficient and result-oriented work that is left. That is an extra 4.8 hours in your work week. Putting it all together, 6 + 4.8 is 10.8 hours. In 10.8 hours, you have managed to accomplish 80 percent of your outcomes, plus another 80 percent of the remaining results. As a result, a massive 96 percent of our true value was done in a mere 10.8 hours (out of the 30)!

This is management. How can these 10.8 hours be optimized? How to know which activities and tasks bring that added value, and how to extract the most out of these tasks? And how to extract value out of the remaining almost 20 hours of the week that lead, under normal circumstances, to less than 4 percent of the outcome and the results?

When I realized this, I started seeing my job quite differently, doing and thinking differently, accomplishing more by focusing on the added value, and often having some time to spare (not always wasting 20 hours on low-value or useless tasks). Instead of laboring away at meaningless tasks, I can take this time to think and ask myself questions such as, *How and what can I do to optimize further and how can I be as efficient during this 'leftover' time, so that much more than 10.8 hours a week bring valuable, powerful results?*

My Definition of a Manager

Efficiency became my obsession. Management, as I defined it above, became my passion. And after seeing others around me going down lists of tasks, putting in long hours, and accomplishing very little, helping them became my calling. My obsession made me study a book called *The Art of War,* which defines, in a competitive landscape, how to win with ease with fewer losses, less waste, and less spending of resources. My passion made me try to apply these efficiency concepts to the managerial world, as well.

This has led me to my very own definition of a manager. You may like it or not, but I try to live by it and when I do, it leads to great outcomes.

A manager is someone who strategically activates resources to achieve their finality with effectiveness and efficiency.

In other words, management is not delegating or doing millions of things just because they are on a list, but smartly using available resources (people, situations, money, time) so that what needs to happen happens, and consequently, so that there are plenty of resources left for other things to happen. This, I believe, is true and applicable regardless of your title: One does not need to be a manager to manage.

CHAPTER 2

MANAGING THE FIGHT-OR-FLIGHT RESPONSE

The Fight-or-Flight Response

THE FLIGHT-OR-FIGHT response is a very well-documented physiological response that we have all experienced at one moment or another when faced with an event, situation, or attack that we perceive or expect to be harmful, either physically or mentally. It is easy to find a definition of this response, but here is one from Harvard Medical School[2]:

"A stressful situation — whether something environmental, such as a looming work deadline, or psychological, such as persistent worry about losing a job — can trigger a cascade of stress hormones that produce well-orchestrated physiological changes. A stressful incident can make the heart pound and breathing quicken. Muscles tense and beads of sweat appear.

This combination of reactions to stress is also known as the "fight-or-flight" response because it evolved as a survival mechanism, enabling people and other mammals

---

2 https://www.health.harvard.edu/staying-healthy/understanding-the-stress-response

to react quickly to life-threatening situations. The carefully orchestrated yet near-instantaneous sequence of hormonal changes and physiological responses helps someone to fight the threat off or flee to safety. Unfortunately, the body can also overreact to stressors that are not life-threatening, such as traffic jams, work pressure, and family difficulties."

In the Workspace

The definition above cites two work-related examples: deadlines and the fear of losing a job. Many other professional events may trigger this response: an interview, a conference in front of a packed (or almost empty) large room, and so on. The situation I would like to focus on, which is very relevant to management as I define it, is a confrontation or argument with a colleague. This confrontation can be with a colleague, but it can also be with an employee, a superior (direct or indirect), a stakeholder (internal or external), a partner, or a supplier. This puts us in a position where we may need to justify, argue, explain, defend, or just take in what is being said.

When we feel the urge to flee or to fight, we are likely confronting someone of relevance who can impact our career, our project, or our job. In other words, somebody who if you agreed with, could be an ally. Let's do a quick look at the two options:

- Flight:
  - Leave frustrated, sad, or any other negative and not very constructive emotion.

- Have hope that things will eventually change (however, hope should not be a strategy).
- Hold on to expectations that this or that will happen (see next chapter for my thoughts on managing expectations).

- Fight:
  - Confront the person and try to prove your point.
  - Depending on your previous relationship and hierarchy levels, this confrontation can have many outcomes, most of which are not likely to be productive.
  - When we fight, we force a point of view. Forcing, whether on people or objects, may eventually lead to a breaking point.

Both reactions do little to strengthen a possible ally relationship.

As mentioned in the previous chapter, I define management as "strategically activating resources." Resources do not necessarily mean subordinates. If this person that generates the flight-or-flight response has the potential to be an ally, now or down the road, they are a resource that can be used and activated strategically. Even if you personally have no authority over this person, the situation always has some sort of authority since situations often dictate our actions. If the situation is such that the person reacts in a way that is beneficial for your goals and strategy, then the resource is activated. But fleeing or fighting does not achieve this.

Therefore, managerially speaking, neither fight nor flight is beneficial.

Ancient Wisdom

I try to apply teachings from Tibetan and Chinese philosophy in my everyday life, and this extends to the way I manage.

So, what does the spiritual leader of Tiber, His Holiness the Dalai Lama[3] teach us in such situations?

*"I defeat my enemies when I **make them my friends**."*[4]

At the opposite end of the thought spectrum, Sun Tzu in *The Art of War,*[5] says:

*"… the skillful leader subdues the enemy's troops **without any fighting** …"* [6]

Fights, arguments, and conflicts do not create friends and allies, and they expend much of our energy. My definition of management states that one must activate resources to achieve finality with *efficiency*. Using copious amounts of emotional energy is far from the efficiency we are looking for.

Let's see what happens if we further explore Tibetan and Chinese philosophy about management.

---

3 https://www.dalailama.com/
4 https://bestdalailamaquotes.tumblr.com/post/100801362862/i-defeat-my-enemies-when-i-make-them-my-friends
5 https://www.goodreads.com/book/show/10534.The_Art_of_War.
6 Translation from Lionel Giles, Chapter III, line 6

The Art of Management

If we can anticipate an upcoming confrontation, it is possible to use the time leading up to this confrontation strategically. Time is the manager's resource that enables them to activate other resources. For example, there are quite often a few minutes of informal chit-chat before a meeting. The manager can use this time to seed outcomes; to "make a friend" as the Dalai Lama says. Show interest in the person that you fear: Ask about their weekend, their family, or their interests. This puts both of you in a relationship of friendship or allyship, and they will be much more reluctant to use confrontational words with a friend or ally. By using the time available, the manager can set up the situation so that it may evolve to be a much more constructive one.

Then, as the meeting progresses, if the anticipated divergence still arises, the best way to proceed is to avoid fighting, as per the advice of Sun Tzu. Accept, agree, and reinforce the position of the other. This will likely take them off guard (they were probably expecting a confrontation as well) and put them in a perceived winning position. This is the moment when you can seed ideas and concepts.

To paraphrase François Jullien in his 2004 essay *A Treatise on Efficacy*:

There is only one way to have the upper hand on the other and make him act as we wish: adapt ourselves to him. It is by constantly conforming ourselves to the other, and therefore never going against him, that we are sure to have no resistance from him. We become a confidante, an ally, and as a result, we can maneuver him. I certify as true what he says, I highlight the essentials, etc. The other therefore evolves into a state of permanent agreement that gradually removes his power and allows us to guide the conversation.

The purpose of speech is not for us to talk, but to get the other one to talk, which allows us to constantly adapt ourselves to him. I talk to make him say. I listen to impose my will. It is by adapting myself to his disposition that I can manage him. I follow him to understand him and eventually, to lead him.

I am not saying that this approach should be used all the time. As a friend of mine often says, "There are no recipes in management." Some situations and proposals are not acceptable and need to be denounced. Nonetheless, this is an approach that has helped me in more than one situation, and it is well worth mentioning.

CHAPTER 3

MANAGING EXPECTATIONS ... OR NOT

The Arts

AS MENTIONED IN MY chapter on the flight-or-fight response, I try as much as possible to follow two schools of thought, both in my personal and professional life. One is based on the Dalai Lama's *The Art of Happiness*, and the other one on Sun Tzu's *The Art of War*.

To many, combining these two schools of thought seems completely nonsensical and dichotomous. One is about peace and happiness and the other one is about war, victory, and defeating the enemy. But sometimes, two opposites come together to form a whole.

Upon closer examination, *The Art of Happiness* teaches us that when you are not calm, when emotions take over, you cannot see clearly, and your judgement is impaired. As a result, you over- or underreact, based on the emotions you are experiencing. *The Art of War*, in one of many examples, tells us, *"The general, unable to control his irritation, will launch his men to the assault like swarming ants, with the result that one-third of his men are slain, while the town remains untaken.*"[7] Emotions cloud our judgment and impair our ability to see the reality of a situation. Therefore, both authors write about seeing things as they are and acting upon that knowledge.

The Art of Happiness is all about conquering internal foes, understanding who we are, how we react, and why we react the way we do. *The Art of War,* on the other hand, is about conquering external foes, understanding who they are, how they react, and why they react the way they do. Both are based on a thorough understanding of the battleground (whether this battleground is our minds or a situation of global warfare). They teach us how to perceive what is there and how to act or react based on this information.

Impacts of Expectations

Let's once again examine the two schools of thought, and then we can try to see how we can apply them to management.

The Dalai Lama's *The Art of Happiness* teaches us that the only thing we control about an event or a situation is our perception of it. Something happens totally out of our control (it rains, for example). How we decide to perceive it and deal with it is the only true control we have. If we have expectations that this or that will happen (for example, that my son will clean his room) and the expectation

---

7 Translation from Lionel Giles, Chapter III, line 5

is not met, it leads to negative emotions, such as frustration, disappointment, jealousy, impatience, sadness, etc. We "outsource" our happiness to external factors, factors over which we have no control. We do not control the weather or the actions of others. Who are we to believe that because we expect the world (or God) to produce a certain path, the world will listen to us and produce it? If the world does satisfy our expectations, we are satisfied, but not overly excited, whereas if it doesn't, then the negative emotions kick in. By controlling how we react to whatever the world is throwing at us, we can decide to react positively and even happily. We can choose to let go of our expectations and accept what comes at us with openness, curiosity, and excitement.

The Art of War teaches us to deepen our external understanding of conflict: it examines the environment of a confrontation (what information does the time and place of a confrontation tell us?), and it helps us evaluate and understand who the other is. *("If you know the enemy and know yourself, you need not fear the result of a hundred battles."*[8]) If we have expectations that this or that will happen, we are not prepared for a different outcome, and we will likely not achieve what we set out to accomplish. Once again, we "outsource" our victory to external factors. Who are we to believe that because we expect someone to say something, they will? How can we be certain

---

8 Translation from Lionel Giles, Chapter III, line 18

that a situation will evolve the way we expect it to? By controlling our understanding of the situation, we control our ability to react and not depend on expectations.

Expectations and Management

So where does this discussion leave us as managers? An approach I have taken and am still learning to apply to my life is to remove all expectations. By "remove," I do not mean simply lowering your expectations; I mean completely removing them. This approach asks you to have no expectations and to be ready to react to whatever comes your way.

This does not mean having no hopes or dreams. It means not planning your next move with the expectation that the hope or dream will occur in the next instant. Also, if you have expectations and a plan for when those expectations are fulfilled, when the situation does not go exactly as you had imagined it, in addition to being disappointed that the world did not cooperate with your desires, the plan you had prepared will have been prepared in vain, as you can no longer apply it to the new situation.

United States President Dwight Eisenhower said in a 1957 speech to the National Defense Executive Reserve Conference: "In preparing for battle I have always found that plans are useless, but planning is indispensable."[9] In light of the present discussion on expectations, this makes

---

9 https://www.presidency.ucsb.edu/documents/remarks-the-national-defense-executive-reserve-conference

perfect sense, as plans very seldom, if ever, go according to how we think they will. Instead of forming a rigid plan, the idea is to understand enough about the situation to give you the flexibility to strategically pivot when changes to the situation arise.

An animated YouTube video that explains *The Art of War*[10], says that on the eve of the battle of Waterloo, Lord Uxbridge went to the Duke of Wellington to find out what his plans were for the upcoming battle because he knew he might find himself commander in chief. The duke asked: "Who will attack first tomorrow, I or Bonaparte?" After Lord Uxbridge confirmed that Bonaparte will attack first, the duke continued: "Well, Bonaparte has not given me any idea of his projects, and as my plans will depend upon his, how can you expect me to tell you what mine are?"

The Duke of Wellington defeated Napoleon at Waterloo, and maybe not having fixed plans played a part in that.

In other words, if the best-possible outcome happens, great. If not, great as well. This alternate outcome opens up new possibilities for anyone who is not burdened by their expectations. Chinese philosophy often refers to the progression of water. Flowing water constantly adapts; it takes the shape of the landscape. Water does not plan or expect, but instead follows the path it encounters and always gets where it needs to go.

---

10 Chapter I, line 9 of The Art of War explained via animation https://www.youtube.com/watch?v=NPpJbOVIUGc

More often than not, expectations lead to judgment of self, of others, of the situation. Judgment blurs reality through our biased lenses...judgment applies a filter on facts.

The efficient manager, by not having any expectations, observes. When you observe you understand; when you understand, you adapt and when you adapt, you can transform. Expectations block all this.

CHAPTER 4

MANAGING GLORY VS. RESULTS

IN THIS CHAPTER, I will go over some interesting statistics about work appreciation, which will be followed by information about the top cause of employee dissatisfaction. I will then examine a strategy that can lead to great managerial opportunities.

The Ping-Pong Example

In a funny LinkedIn Post[11], there is a fantastic video of an elderly man playing Ping-Pong with someone younger. The elderly man barely takes a single step in the entire exchange; however, he positions the ball so that his opponent is almost running a marathon. While this is a hilarious video, I like the fact that it shows managerial efficiency: less effort with top results.

Under that post about the Ping-Pong video, one of my LinkedIn contacts had the same idea as I did and commented: "Not spectacular, though much more valuable than

---

11 https://www.linkedin.com/posts/francis-audet-6917183_work-exercise-activity-6696363530897154048-YUy1

tons of heroic actions (unless you're just selling a show)." I replied: "Winning with ease brings no praise and glory, as everything seems simple, but delivers results. The question is, as managers, which one is more important: glory or results?"

Let's return to my definition of a manager: someone who strategically activates resources to reach his finality with effectiveness and efficiency. The emphasis here is clearly on the importance of the results. But what about glory?

My LinkedIn contact answered my question in this way: "I would tend to say the answer to your last question might depend on 1- Which outcome does your organization reward and encourage (through promotion, money, celebration, or any other incentives) and 2- What are you trying to achieve as a manager." Well, as a manager, I try to achieve finality with efficiency. Period.

The Bane of the Office

A Gallup poll[12] showed that a staggering 85 percent of people hate their job. The rate is slightly better in some countries (like the United States, where only 70 percent of people hate their jobs) and worse in others. Different studies have different results, depending on how the question is asked and how one defines "liking your job." For example, the US Conference Board[13] found that 50 percent of workers were unhappy with their job in 2019. But regardless of the study, even the most optimistic number (50 percent of the

---

12 https://returntonow.net/2017/09/22/85-people-hate-jobs-gallup-poll-says/
13 https://www.conference-board.org/press/pressdetail.cfm?pressid=9160

entire workforce) remains an enormous number of people. Other surveys and studies that try to understand why this is the case come to a similar conclusion.

The Gallup poll article cited mentions that, according to Forbes, "The most obvious fix for unhappy workers" is communication, praise, and encouragement: "Tell them what you expect of them, praise them when they do well, encourage them to move forward. Give them the tools they need and the opportunity to feel challenged."

Forbes global studies[14] reveal that 79 percent of people who quit their jobs cite "lack of appreciation" as their reason for leaving. Recognition is the number one thing employees say their manager could give them to inspire them to produce great work. Global studies prove that when it comes to inspiring people to be their best at work, nothing else comes close — not even higher pay, promotion, autonomy, or training.

We can look at Maslow's Hierarchy of Needs, a classification system intended to reflect the universal needs of society as its base then proceed to more acquired emotions to help pinpoint the struggle area. Proposed by American Abraham Maslow in his 1943 paper "A Theory of Human Motivation" and published in the journal *Psychological Review*, it states that belongingness and love, then prestige, esteem, and a feeling of accomplishment are the needs that come right after safety and security.

---

14 https://www.forbes.com/sites/davidsturt/2018/03/08/10-shocking-workplace-stats-you-need-to-know/?sh=5084a500f3af

If these needs are not being addressed, then high self-esteem and self-actualization (both of which are required to be happy) are out of reach.

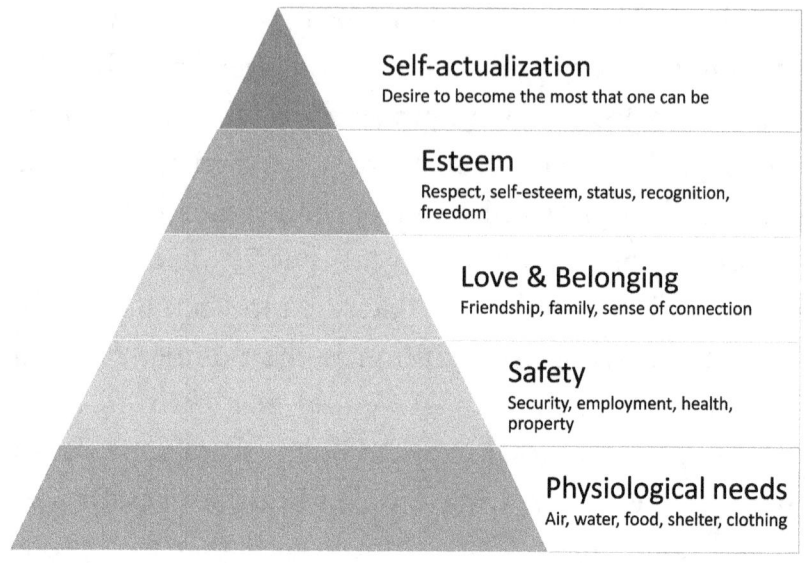

Figure 1: Maslow's Hierarchy of Need

A team or a company can have fantastic results; however, if an employee is not praised, they will likely not love their job. So, there we have it: Glory and recognition surpass results for most people. Results seem to matter less than the fact of being acknowledged for that result.

The Glory Seeker

In *The Art of War*, Sun Tzu says in Chapter 4: "Neither is it the acme of excellence if you fight and conquer and the whole Empire says, 'Well done!' What the ancients called a clever fighter is one who not only wins but excels in winning with ease. Hence his victories bring him neither reputation for wisdom nor credit for courage."[15] Here, the ancient warrior is not a glory seeker, but instead a victory seeker, a result seeker. They are obsessed with results and victory, not with self-pride. Sun Tzu goes on to conclude that if the general is seen as a hero if they save the day and get recognition, it is because the plan was flawed, and a heroic last-minute action needed to occur. If the acorn is planted, eventually, the oak will grow. There is no need for heroism. This way of thinking does not achieve glory, but it does achieve results.

Managing Glory

Where then does that leave us as managers? We know:

- We have human resources at our disposal under either our direct or indirect influence.
- A big proportion of those employees likely do not love their jobs.
- They long for praise, recognition, and acknowledgement.
- We, as managers, should be obsessed with results, not self-glory.

Now, it just so happens that praise, glory, acknowledgment, and recognition are free to give. It is in our power

---

15 Translation from Lionel Giles, Chapter IV, lines 9, 11 and 12

to help our direct resources (our employees), and even our indirect resources (please refer to Chapters 2 and 39 for examples, and a definition of indirect resources), move up the Maslow pyramid. The more we fulfill these needs, the more engaged they will be, and the more likely it is that they will follow our lead. While leadership and management are different, leadership is a good tool for a manager to have. Good leadership leads to good followership. Put your resources at the forefront: Give them the prestige and the recognition they long for, and they will reward you tenfold.

One may ask the question: Where does that leave the manager if they always give credit, do not seek glory for themselves, and do not self-praise? Well, that leaves them in a position where they always succeed: Their projects are always delivered, their numbers are always met, and their retention rate is higher. They do not seek glory; they seek and deliver results, and companies live or die on results. Companies, therefore, live or die on efficient management.

I have seen many managers who try to make themselves believe they are result seekers, yet want their names circulated and praised. It is hard to be both a glory seeker and a result seeker since glory is individual and results are a consequence of many subtle elements. Which one do you, as a manager, want to be?

CHAPTER 5

MANAGING THE RECIPE

MIX FLOUR, EGGS, and milk following a certain ratio and you get pancake batter. Do that today or tomorrow, and you still get pancake batter. Do that in Canada, Japan, or South Africa, and guess what? You still get pancake batter. Why does it work and why is it repeatable? Well, quite simply, regardless of what time it is or where you are, those three ingredients are pretty much always the same. This is what we call a recipe.

However, this is not a book about cooking.

What About Managerial Recipes?

Sun Tzu called his teachings *The Art of War*, not *The Recipe for War*, not *The Guide to Always Win in 12 Steps*. Managing victory and progress is an art. His entire Chapter 7 is based on that: Adapt to the situation. The situation, not the plan, dictates the next move. So, whether you are trying to accelerate a project, improve a process, get your team to do something, or just comfort someone in distress to help them get better, these are all situations to manage. *The Art of War* tells us that there is no "one size fits all."

In human relationships, I would dare say that there is not even a "one size fits twice."

Everything that is done to successfully manage any of the situations above, or any other situation that may occur, was successful because of the conditions that were present at that moment. I could list specific conditions for a long time: The ambiance, the mental state of all parties involved, and the environment are just some of the factors involved.

"My project is struggling, and last time I solved such a struggle doing *xyz*; let's re-do that." This type of thinking is something I see and witness repeatedly. People use past successes and copy and paste them, hoping that the results will be the same. However, reality has changed. People, situations, objectives, and backgrounds change continuously. They are not eggs, flour, and milk in a fixed ratio.

You will tell me, "This is all so obvious." So then why is there this constant repeat of recipes when managing or implementing change? Here are a few reasons I hear:

- This is the elevator pitch and how a product "should" be sold.
- This is an organizational structure that management deploys across the company.
- We need to be fair and treat all our employees the same.
- All our projects will be based on Agile software development[16].

---

16 https://www.techtarget.com/searchsoftwarequality/definition/agile-software-development

The role of the manager is determined by the circumstances. It is by being constantly fluid, available, and flexible that we can continuously adapt to the situation. There are, in my opinion, few worse things for a manager that wishes to be efficient than to restrict oneself to rules and apply recipes. This fixes behavior and restrains them from seeing and understanding the uniqueness of the current context. They always need to be in harmony with the renewal of the situation.

The Liquid Manager

In Chapter 3, I mentioned that Chinese philosophy often refers to water progressing: water constantly adapts and takes the shape of the landscape. Water does not plan or expect, but instead follows whatever the landscape has to offer and gets where it needs to go in this way.

In a great Ted Talk on the subject,[17] Raymond Tang highlights his "Lessons of Water." Some of his words apply to this discussion:

1. "Water always gets where it needs to go without war or conflict. When water flows toward a rock, it goes around it. Whatever the obstacle, somehow, water finds a solution, without force, without conflict. Better to work in harmony with our environment."

---

17 https://www.ted.com/talks/raymond_tang_be_humble_and_other_lessons_from_the_philosophy_of_water?language=en

2. "Water is open to change and has no fixed shape or state of mind. It constantly adapts effortlessly to any circumstances."

There are no recipes for water's progress.

The following quote is attributed to Albert Einstein[18] (although I love Bart Simpson's usage of it[19]): "Insanity is doing the same thing over and over and expecting different results." Water never does the same thing twice; it constantly adapts.

To refer again to Sun Tzu: "Water shapes its course according to the nature of the ground over which it flows; the soldier works out his victory about the foe whom he is facing. Therefore, just as water retains no constant shape, so in warfare there are no constant conditions. He who can modify his tactics about his opponent and thereby succeed in winning, may be called a heaven-born captain."[20]

If a soldier can adapt based on their enemy, then maybe a manager can modify their approach and their actions to their team and their project.

So as managers, instead of relying on our known approaches and recipes, why not use the conclusion of Raymond Tang's speech: When faced with a challenge, ask yourself: What would Water do …?

---

18 Goodreads.com, Albert Einstein Quotes
19 https://www.youtube.com/watch?v=bYJQPYKvU6U
20 Translation from Lionel Giles, Translation from Lionel Giles, Chapter VI, lines 31-33

CHAPTER 6

MANAGING TALENT

HAVE YOU EVER HEARD the expression "Square peg in a round hole"? Dictionary.com describes it as "A misfit, especially a person unsuited for a position or activity."[21] There will always be square pegs and round holes: Everyday situations constantly require you to face a challenge or an opportunity that you have never faced before, and this makes you feel powerless or like an impostor. You need to do something, react, or act and you simply don't have the skill set or the experience to do it smoothly and flawlessly. You may very well feel like square pegs trying to squeeze into a round hole. Often, though, because of your past experiences and your adaptability, you learn and you manage to eventually overcome the situation you are presented with. In the workplace, how can this process be smoothed out to be more efficient?

Finding the Right Peg

Have you ever been in a situation of hiring someone or being hired? The candidate, whether it was you or someone

---

21 https://www.dictionary.com/browse/square-peg-in-a-round-hole

you interviewed, had potential, experience, and talent, all of which were displayed during the hiring process. Then, the candidate was hired for the job. And, of course, the tasks and responsibilities did not 100 percent match the talent of the individual, but they were so good and had so much potential, that they just had to be hired. The peg is *almost* round.

And then corporate pressure, or a narrow-minded boss, tried to fit the greatest almost-round peg (made of pure gold, and impossible to ignore or miss out on) into a round hole.

People are hired for their talent, and for what they can bring to the table. Why, once hired, do we either, due to authority, lack of vision, or insecurity, ignore or fail to exploit the very reason the individual was hired? Why try to shape the diamond we have hired to fit the hole we had previously defined, instead of adapting the hole to the shape of the peg?

We think, "Man, this candidate is such a great strategist and visionary...Let's go with him," and this same individual ends up a few months later in an operational job.

Why not let the talented bird sing in all its glory?

Jack vs. Master

People are great at what they love, and they love what they are great at. The efficient manager needs to recognize that "what a person loves and what they are great at" is in their resource network and they need to tap into that potential as much as possible. The more a manager does this, the more they will advance toward their goal.

If an employee does nothing of what is in their textbook job definition, yet they deliver tremendous value and achieve the results that the job description strives for, will you allow them to innovate and modify their approach so that more value is created, or will you tell them, "I want you to do more of this and that" because this is how such a person in this position should behave?

Let's say, for example, a job definition has two main components. The new employee is incredible at one of them, the best in the business, but they are not very skilled in the second component. A few choices are in front of us:

1. Move on and do not hire them since the peg is not the proper shape.
   o This means missing out on one of the best options for a critical part of the mandate and therefore settling for less talent in this particular aspect.
2. Hire and train/force the individual to perform both roles since this is the job definition.
   o The result here will be an employee who around 50 percent of the time does not feel good enough. They will be performing a task they do not enjoy and will likely never meet their boss' expectations.

3. Split the role and get the new hire to focus on what they excel at.

   o This option leads to an energized employee who becomes world-class in their discipline/field and brings your business to the next level.

Some jobs require a jack-of-all-trades, but this person is often a master of none. If you have a master at something, it is very unlikely you will transform them into a master of everything. By attempting to do so, they will become a jack-of-all-trades. Pele or Messi were/are not the best in the world because they were asked to improve their defensive skills. Their talent was to score and generate goals, and that is what was/is asked of them.

As efficient managers, we must, therefore, be able to recognize the specific potential in each of our resources, direct and indirect, and make sure we tap into that talent. The value generated in this way will be much higher: They will remain engaged and their willingness to help you will increase tenfold. I like to call this "Role vs. Function," which I will discuss in depth in Chapter 25.

A manager's function is to achieve a certain result. Their role should be defined by the circumstances. Those circumstances include many resources that each has their unique skills and talents. The more the manager will tap into those, the more likely their goal will be achieved with ease. Don't be so stubborn as to believe that everyone must fit into what is called the "job definition," or the shape of the hole. Remember my section on water in the previous chapter: Water has no shape and adapts to the environment presented to it. Why then should we force resources, employees, and talented individuals to assume a permanent shape that differs from their natural one? Instead, why not adapt your requirements, your strategy, and your path to victory to what the landscape offers?

CHAPTER 7

MANAGING SUCCESS

SO, WHAT IS SUCCESS? Cambridge Dictionary defines it as: *"the achieving of the results wanted or hoped for."*[22] Hope can be linked to expectations. I have already discussed my thoughts on expectations in Chapter 3. If one manages to remove all expectations, as I recommended, and is ready to react to whatever comes their way, then this definition does not help us define our success and it can be quite hard to manage something that we cannot define.

Success is relative. Everybody defines their success differently, either because they reflected and developed their own measure of success or, more often, because they "borrowed" the idea of success from somewhere else (for example, from their parents or society). Because of this, for many, success has to do with visible accomplishments: a healthy and prosperous family, a prestigious job, a big house, and expensive cars. In other words, things that can be shown off. For others, success comes from the mastery of a discipline or the winning of awards and medals. In all

---

22 https://dictionary.cambridge.org/dictionary/english/success

these examples, success is measured in comparison to others. We outsource our ability to feel successful partly to how others perceive us and to how we perform compared to them.

A Different Definition of Success

What if we defined success as the mastery of oneself instead?

Under the blog posts that I used to have, I received the two following comments:

- "Having expectations leads to emotional responses (good or bad it does not matter) that blur the broader view. Often you need a signal to guide yourself that does not activate the emotional part but acts as a neutral compass to know where you are."
- "Very interesting post that clearly explains that our knee-jerk, natural response to difficult situations, that is to fight or flight, is deeply rooted in our physiology. I like the way you describe there is a better, third way to handle difficult situations, that can even possibly help build better relationships at the same time, setting us up for future success."

The above comments point to the fact that we are looking for inner signals; we are searching for a purposeful way to act that goes against the natural physiological response. Both strategies lead to self-awareness. Every action we make comes from a thought or an intention, conscious or not (most often unconscious). It, therefore, makes a lot of sense to pay attention to what type of thoughts we are cultivating (or at least trying to cultivate). Every decision creates change and helps us develop in a direction, which can lead us to a better or worse position. The more aware we become of this, and of where these changes take place, the more we can influence and cultivate them. When we feed our physical body with junk food instead of healthy food, regardless of all other actions being taken to alter the body, the body will suffer and deteriorate. So, what happens then to our mind when we feed it junk thoughts? If we give our minds problems, sorrows, stress, conflict, hate, and greed to eat, how will our thoughts develop and how will our minds change?

The Dalai Lama defines the purpose of life as finding happiness[23]. Now we may not all agree with this, but let's explore a path in which happiness is, in fact, the goal of life. If this happiness depends on external successes, on what people think about us, tell us, on the size of our house, on the number on our paycheck, or on what circumstances bring, then we are outsourcing our happiness to sources we do not control. If we let outside sources affect us inside, who then is in control of our life? Instead of trying to control the outside to please us, why not try to control the only single being we can control: ourselves? The more we understand ourselves, the better we will be at finding and

---

23 Goodreads.com, Dalai Lama XIV Quotes

listening to the signals described in the comments above, and the better we will be at controlling our emotions, our reactions, our thoughts, and, consequently, our actions and decisions. Our happiness remains in our control instead of relying on the praise and behaviors of others.

Humility and Ego

On this path of self-mastery and of understanding and controlling our thoughts, success can now easily be defined. Every moment when we control our thoughts, our responses, and our actions instead of delivering de-facto, reflex-based responses is a success. And like everything else, the more one tries, the better they become. No one remains in complete control all the time, but there is always improvement and new successes to celebrate. The path to self-mastery is a continuum, not a binary measure. This differs from most external success metrics or key performance indicators (KPIs). "I have a great job, I bought the latest great car, I won the competition." One problem with these metrics is: and then what? To feel once again successful, you need a better job, a better car, and to win more competitions. Additionally, this neverending cycle comes with stress, pressure, and expectations.

On this path of self-mastery, one forever remains an apprentice, meaning one always looks for lessons, answers, and improvements, and these can come from any place, even the most unexpected ones. It is a question of putting ourselves into a certain state of mind. We are always students, or apprentices, and everybody and everything can teach us something. Hence, everybody and everything become our master (master here refers to the "master" as defined by the master-apprentice relationship[24]), and we become theirs as well. A great master knows he will forever be an apprentice, and the great apprentice knows he is surrounded by masters.

But this is not an easy road: We get very little outside praise (as discussed in my chapter on Glory Seekers[25]). The ego will starve, and humility must become our guide. We must look inside ourselves for solutions, signals, and gratification. We tend to put a lot of time and effort into developing skills (business skills, negotiation skills, sports, music, tinkering), but what about time spent on improving who we are and what we are? What about time spent on how we control our thoughts, and ultimately, how we can become a better person? (As Gandhi put it, "Be the change that you wish to see in the world."[26]) It takes self-discipline to evolve toward self-mastery, but self-discipline leads to self-responsibility, which also eventually leads to self-care and then to self-love. This is the path to take to find success and happiness from within.

In this way, we can manage success and our own lives completely. And in this way, we can see, act, react,

24 https://thunder-university.medium.com/introducing-the-master-apprentice-model-for-the-modern-age-2aa1006e1e77
25 Chapter 4
26 Goodreads.com, Mahatma Gandhi Quotes

and interact with efficiency, and clarity. We can manage efficiently.

To quote the Shaolin master Shi Heng Yi: "There are two mistakes along the path to self-mastery: Not starting it and not going all the way."[27]

---

27 https://www.shihengyi.online/#:~:text=%22There%20are%20two%20mistakes%20 along, way%20towards%20 your%20own%20destiny.

CHAPTER 8

MANAGING THE CORNERED CAT

WHAT WILL A CORNERED cat typically do? Show teeth, ready its claws, and prepare to fight, even if the threat he faces is much stronger and the odds are against him. That is unless there is a way out that will lead back to safety and that will avoid the fight.

As managers, what can we learn from this?

The Art of Cat War

In *The Art of War*, Sun Tzu says: "When you surround an army, leave an outlet free. Do not press a desperate foe too hard."[28]

Here, the enemy is like the cornered cat. If the opponent is pressed too much, it will go to any length to avoid perishing and will fight with the energy of desperation. This type of behavior puts our position at risk and requires more effort and more resources to defeat the opponent, win the argument, or make the sale, for

---

28 Translation from Lionel Giles, Chapter XII, line 36

example. And as an efficient manager who wants to opti-mize results with minimal resources and waste, this is not the best tactic.

To further his point, Sun Tzu explains that he likes his troops to be cornered because he knows this will produce the greatest fight in them: "Throw your soldiers into posi-tions whence there is no escape, and they will prefer death to flight. If they will face death, there is nothing they may not achieve. Officers and men alike will put forth their uttermost strength. Soldiers when in desperate straits lose the sense of fear. If there is no place of refuge, they will stand firm. If they are in hostile country, they will show a stubborn front. If there is no help for it, they will fight hard."[29]

This quote insinuates that he fears his opponents will use his strategy against him: He fears the opposing army will provide his troops with an escape route, knowing this method will encourage his troops to avoid conflict and therefore give his opponent the advantage. Of course, in the corporate managerial world, we do not want to put our team in a do-or-die situation. Furthermore, we do not combat foes, we work with allies.

So then, taking these differences into account, how can we apply this strategy? And why still provide an alternate route for the cat to escape or for the opposing army to flee to safety?

---

29 Translation from Lionel Giles, Chapter XI, lines 23-24

Letting the Effect Occur

The cat will flee to safety (or in the case of a managerial situation, to a result unwanted by the manager) if he can find an escape route that had not already been planned by the manager. However, if the exit door has been planned and seeded ahead of time by a skillful manager, then it is quite easy to predict what the cornered cat will do. It becomes possible to control the outcome of what the cat believes is an exit. In *The Art of War*, the concept of efficiency is defined by the ability to have an effect occur naturally and by itself. If we are going by this and would like to manage as efficiently as possible, then we should not aim at producing an effect directly (we do not push the cat to the open exit), but we should instead imply the intended effect by setting up the situation so that the result naturally occurs (we would like the cat to believe he found the exit himself and choose it without us applying any force). As such, if one does not fight it is not because he wants to remove himself from the situation, but to better succeed by letting the effect play itself out, deciding where the cat will go and therefore the outcome of the situation.

Foe vs. Ally

So far in this discussion about the cornered cat and *The Art of War*, we have been referencing a conflict and the cat represents a foe to defeat. However, most managerial situations do not involve a foe but an ally, a colleague, a partner, a supplier, or a customer. These are not people we want to corner and defeat. Nonetheless, these are often people whom we need to act and behave a certain way in certain situations to achieve our goals.

The strategy of the cornered cat is at its best in situations when these allies have taken an action (or inaction) that is detrimental to our progress. They have done something wrong, such as omitting something, and this should not have been, and must ideally not happen again. Confrontation will often force a situation that may lead to breaking points and dictating with authority can often be ill-perceived, and alienating our allies is of no interest to us.

So, instead of dictating the path one should have taken, instead of pushing the cat in the exit, the manager must imply it so that the effect may occur naturally. If we not only understand our finality, but theirs as well, it should be quite simple to point out what was wrong, misdone, or misplaced, and highlight the sour impact on not only our own objectives but on theirs as well. In such a situation, the other can fight, argue, or simply offer up a solution. They can suggest something they will do differently next time and say something like: "You're right, I'm sorry. Next time I will do this and that and don't hesitate to let me know if there's anything else I can do differently." In other words, they are taking the escape route to avoid the fight. This is an escape door that you did not dictate, but that naturally flowed from the situation, and that they believe they found on their own.

If, for example, as a manager, you are not informed of something critical for your project, instead of confronting and saying things such as, "You should have told me," or "In the future be sure to inform me," try the cornered cat approach, which is much more subtle. It could go something like this: "I wish I would have known, as it would have allowed me to do this or that, which would have helped you achieve a certain goal." This kind of formulation mentions the wrongdoing without seeming accusatory. The other then recognizes they are cornered (recognizes their fault) and will naturally suggest doing something different next time (they found the door to safety, the one that you created but did not force them into).

All actions, or circumstances encountered, invite us into the situation, from where it is much easier to seed and shape future outcomes. The potential to shape the situation, in this case, comes from something that was done in contradiction to our goals. And so, the wheel turns: circumstances continue to generate potential, which leads to new circumstances, and also, to constantly renewed potential.

CHAPTER 9

MANAGING FROM WITHIN

THE BEST, AND MAYBE the only way to influence a situation efficiently is to be in the situation. Police infiltrate to dismantle criminal organizations, just as bad guys infiltrate to influence corporations or political organizations. You can complain all you want about politicians or sports athletes from the comfort of your living room, and it might even feel good to do so, but that won't change anything about the situation itself. To go vote or to go to the venue where your team is playing gives you a little bit of power. Not a lot, but your ability to influence is already more than when you remain a bystander. Getting involved opens up the possibility to change things from within.

But it is not always easy to get involved, especially in a corporate or work environment. Let's say, as a manager, you hear a rumor that this or that subject is being discussed, and this subject would contribute to your ability to perform your job, yet you are not in the loop. What kind of leverage or power do you have on the evolution and outcome of that subject?

On the other hand, if such a situation occurs and you decide to "crash in," or ask questions to understand and start to influence, the other party can become defensive. This type of intervention can often create a situation where the other party does not know how to react, and their first thought may be: "Did I mess up? Why are they asking this?" This approach, just like crashing in a party uninvited, creates unwelcomeness and potentially awkward situations. Yet, not getting involved and waiting for the information to arrive on its own can take forever.

The simplest, most efficient way is to get invited.

The Siege vs. the Trojan Horse

There are three basic tactics we can use when information is being shared, strategies are being discussed, and we are willingly or not kept out of the loop:

- Wait it out and hope eventually they will realize we are being left out and invite us or hope the situation will progress in our desired direction without our intervention.
- Force our way into the situation.
- Get invited into it.

To reference Sun Tzu's *The Art of War*, in Chapter 3 he writes: "The highest form of generalship is to balk the enemy's plans; the next best is to prevent the junction of the enemy's forces; the next in order is to attack the enemy's army in the field; and the worst policy of all is to besiege walled cities...Therefore, the skillful leader subdues the enemy's troops without any fighting; he captures their cities without laying siege to them."[30]

What he is saying here is that siege, meaning "waiting it out," takes forever, and is not efficient. Confrontation, while faster, can be costly. To balk the plans means to influence the plans; to know about them; to be aware of the situation; to be within the plans to influence them.

The Trojan Horse story[31] is a great example of getting invited into the city and once inside, begin influencing, a strategy the Greeks adopted after a ten-year siege. (Trojan Horse refers to a wooden horse said to have been used by the Greeks during the Trojan War in the Bronze Age, to enter the city of Troy. After the long and fruitless siege, the Greeks constructed a huge wooden horse and hid a select force of men inside. The Greeks pretended to sail away, and the Trojans pulled the horse into their city as a victory trophy. That night the Greek force crept out of the horse and opened the gates for the rest of the Greek army, which had sailed back under cover of night. The Greeks entered and destroyed the city of Troy, ending the war.)

Getting Invited and Working From Within

Now it may not always be easy to get invited to the exact situation we aim to influence. The Greeks did not get invited to overtake Troy: They got invited inside the walls,

---

30 Translation from Lionel Giles, Chapter III, lines 3 and 6
31 https://www.britannica.com/topic/Trojan-horse

into the heart of the city. Once inside, the "Trojan reality or intimacy," it becomes quite simple to steer the conversation toward the desired subject. Once inside the walls, the defences are down, and potential arises.

To illustrate this more concretely, let's take an example. A product line manager (PLM) gets asked by a salesperson what is the unique selling proposition in a given scenario because a customer is inquiring. This is an invitation from the salesperson: He is inviting the PLM into his world or "within his walls." It is likely quite easy for the PLM to give a straight answer and be done with it (therefore closing the door on the invitation extended by the salesperson), but here are a few other options:

- Call the salesperson up to learn more about this customer and the market dynamics they see from their position in the company; gather intelligence. Use this basic question to engage deeper with the person. Maybe use this opportunity to understand how he sells the product, or how his organization is doing; check out what's brewing and what's influenceable. Once inside, the skillful manager steers to their liking.
- Take this opportunity to connect with the customer: Say something like, "It depends. Can you facilitate a call with the customer, so I understand more about the inquiry?" This allows the manager to gather market intel once again, this time from the customer's perspective. From this position, the manager can influence the customer's decisions, get direct

access to final users, and once in there, they can even generate an opportunity to obtain other names, other applications, and so forth.

- Pretend you don't know the answer and go ask someone else, a person from research and development (R&D), for example. Not only does this make the person feel smart and important, but once the discussion is open, once you have managed to be invited into their world, you can use this time to share your roadmap, your vision, or your suggestions for the next product release or implementation.

As can you see, the point is not the answer to the initial question itself, but how you can use this question, this invitation into another's reality, to influence a situation, to set things in motion, or to gather information, which is sometimes not even related to the initial question. This strategy allows us to do all these things without waiting for that information to magically arrive, or without forcing a confrontation. The initial question is but a pretext that allows us to be invited within the walls, defenses lowered, with total trust.

Every manager at every level and in every department receives questions and gets such situational invitations. When this happens, defenses are down, openness is granted, and once inside, then we can begin influencing or steering the discussion in our desired direction and all of this becomes much more fluid and efficient than if we attempt to wait, or to force.

If we remain outside of the situation, all we can do is cling to our expectations, beliefs, and assumptions (we hope or believe the situation will evolve in one way or another) or try to force (impose by authority) our will onto the situation to change it. Both situations are bound to fail:

- Building our plan based on expectations means we believe that reality will go as we wish, and that reality will follow our will. Obviously, situations will very seldom unfold precisely as we hoped they will, and we will continuously be disappointed, destabilized, and a few steps behind, constantly trying to catch up. All this puts us in a state of frustration, anger, or sadness, which will cloud our judgment and skew our actions.
- Imposing our will forces an unnatural progression of things, like pulling on a plant for it to grow faster. Force eventually makes things break.

Every opportunity and every conversation is an open door to manage. Your boss asks for a report: opportunity. Your colleague talks about his weekend: an invitation into his world. As long as we are outside the situation, we can only watch what happens. The situation unfolds in front of our eyes, and we can try to act from the outside, but the only way to truly understand the situation is to be within it. The efficient manager does not passively stay out of things, merely looking at events, and subsequently complaining or issuing orders. They get invited into other people's reality, subtly, and then they plant seeds; they manage.

CHAPTER 10

MANAGING SELF-MASTERY

HAVE YOU EVER SEEN videos of Shaolin monks? Notice how when they take a stance, they seem to be as strong and sturdy as mountains, yet seconds later, they perform feats of agility that seem beyond human capability? They go from being incredibly sturdy and stable to being as fluid as water. They have mastered body and mind probably better than any other. Let's explore these two facets of their mental/physical mastery from a managerial point of view.

There is a sentence in their teachings that can help us with this exploration: "To have a strong back yet a soft front."

Strong Back, Soft Front

Our back is our spine: it is what keeps us strong, upright, and able to confront resistance. It is what was described as the "mountain" in the introduction above.

To have a "strong back" managerially speaking means several things, some of which I touched upon in past chapters such as not seeking the hero's role (Chapter 4), overcoming the fight-or-flight response, and managing instead (Chapter 2). Here are the two main components needed to have a strong back as a manager, summarized:

- Being outwardly strong: This is your ability to be reliable; to be someone your team members, your allies, your friends, and your colleagues can lean on and depend on. This includes promoting and showing in your behavior strength, courage, and dedication. How you manage and lead will affect the followership you receive.
- Being inwardly strong: This is your ability to face adversity, and not get demoralized, and demotivated by events external to yourself. To be inwardly strong, you must have a certain mastery over your thoughts, mind, and spirit; you must show resilience.

It takes a tremendously strong "back" to remain upright amid challenging conditions. Having a strong back does not mean wishing for fewer challenges, but instead means wishing for more wisdom. This wisdom is obtained by facing these challenges and it will in turn aid when facing the next challenge. Being strong calls upon values of equanimity, and it requires being in a state of psychological stability and composure that is undisturbed by the experience of emotions, pain, or other phenomena that may cause others to lose their balance and peace of mind.

To have a "soft front" from the perspective of the manager means to be open to the world and to have compassion. Examples of this include listening to others and going out of your way to help colleagues, friends, and allies with their problems (see the previous chapter on managing talent for an example). Compassion means understanding the pain and the difficulties experienced by others so that you can help them effectively, yet, at the same time, maintain your energy and not be drained by these pains and difficulties. This is where mastery of thoughts and emotions is crucial. Compassion does not drain energy; it empowers us and transmits energy to those around us.

Leadership and Followership

Sun Tzu talks all about the "strong back and soft front" in *The Art of War*. In the very first chapter, he says: "The Commander stands for the virtues of wisdom, sincerity, benevolence, courage, and strictness."[32]

The sincerity and benevolence reference the "soft front." To believe in yourself, to believe in others, and to believe in your approach falls under "sincerity," while helping those you could hinder to create new allies for example and exemplifies benevolence and compassion. Courage and strictness, on the other hand, make up the "strong back." These virtues refer to retaining strictness, reliability, and dependability. The "wisdom"

---

32 Translation from Lionel Giles, Chapter I, line 9

aspect puts it all together: it enables you to understand the reality and to understand not only your position but the other's as well, to create a global reality that guides you and helps you succeed.

These virtues give us our moral compass, or what Sun Tzu calls the Moral Law. He says this Moral Law "causes the people to be in complete accord with their ruler so that they will follow him regardless of their lives, undismayed by any danger."[33]

The moral compass is a unifying state of being, capable of aligning the manager to the employee and vice versa. With it, good leadership leads to good followership.

The Mountain, the Water, and Self Mastery

So, a manager that embodies the mountain is reliable, sturdy, and stable in the face of adversity, and this creates, amongst other things, confidence and trust in their leadership. The manager that embodies the water welcomes, adapts, feels, and demonstrates compassion. Water is needed as much as the mountain as without water, there would be no life. But these do not come from nowhere: mindfulness and self-discipline are required to explore and embark on this journey; on this trail that goes deep into the lake and to the very summit of the mountain. Those who embark upon this journey start to understand that this process is synonymous with cultivating the self.

---

33 Translation from Lionel Giles, Chapter I, lines 5-6

It then becomes irrelevant whether you call it "leisure" or "work" because someone who finds joy in cultivating oneself will continue to pursue the journey of self-improvement regardless of if it is accomplished at home or in the job space.

CHAPTER 11

MANAGING
THE CORPORATE ENTITIES

THERE ARE THREE FUNDAMENTAL entities that any business-oriented organization must satisfy to be prosperous. Ignore one, and the ride to success may be bumpy. Ignore two, and you are likely doomed. Let's explore what these entities are, and how the efficient manager can use this knowledge to take advantage of the situation and put their efforts where they are most needed.

The Financer, the Buyer, and the Maker

Any organization needs funds: money to grow the organization, to invest, and develop. This for a start-up can be a bank, a private investment, venture capital, or maybe even government loans. If a company has a nice portfolio of patents and intellectual property (IP), this can attract large industry player investors that hope to eventually profit from those patents. For larger enterprises, funds can come from Wall Street and the stock market. Regardless of the origin, someone, or something, is putting money forward not because of their generosity or the pretty eyes of the owner, but because they want to generate a profit in the long run. These are called the financers. In a company, often the chief financial officer (CFO) will be obsessed with satisfying this group. They will likely have ways in which to measure their success or metrics such as investment revenues, earnings before interest, taxes, depreciation or amortization (EBITDA), valuation, and margins.

Financers need to have paybacks eventually. They need to see technology, products, and services being developed but, more importantly, sold. From these sales come daily profits and an eventual return on the financers' investments. At some stage, the company needs customers to bring in recurrent cash flow, not only to help the organization survive and be profitable but also to honor and please the financers. These customers that generate cashflow are the buyers. People from the sales department are typically the most involved in pleasing this second entity. Top-line sales, year-over-year (YOY) growth, and market share prices are typical metrics for levels of buyer satisfaction.

Finally, there are the makers. This last entity is everyone who serves and helps build, create, and distribute the service or product that the buyers will give money for. In other words, the makers are primarily (yet not exclusively) the employees of the company, paid of course with the money received from the financers and the cash flow generated by the buyers. Normally, the human resources department deals with this last entity. Employee retention levels are a great metric example that is often used by this department.

Just as a three-legged table stands firm, if you keep your financers, your buyers, and your makers happy and in line, the company will very likely flourish. But just as the table collapses if a leg is removed, neglect an entity and all your hard work could come crashing down.

Who Cares About What?

The efficient manager recognizes these three entities, and he also recognizes who, both in the chain of people in command, but also in the makers they work with, prioritizes one of these groups over another. The efficient manager can spot imbalances in their network, and among their resources (as a group but also as individuals) that can break the harmony between the three groups and lead to frustration, waste, disappointment, and much worse.

Let's say, for example, that, in an extreme case, most of the corporate suite (C-Suite) and the vice presidents (VPs) eat, drink, and dream of the same entity. The efficient manager needs to be able to see this to adapt their speech when they interact with the C-Suite, but also to know which group to focus on to compensate for the disparity and restore the balance. If not, the members of the neglected group in their team will feel left out, neglected, and they will lose interest in the job. This is where the efficient manager can restore balance. Here, the manager has the opportunity to show compassion and care towards a certain entity if the higher management is neglecting it. For example, promote care for your buyers if they are not being given the proper care and recognition.

An efficient manager balances their decisions and interventions. Depending on what a situation requires, sometimes a decision will favor one leg but neglect the other. The attitude is adapted to the reality of the situation and interventions do not always equally include all three entities, but it is important that they do not always favor, or neglect, the same entity.

Observation and Compensation

With this in mind, and by observing the attitude of some managers, directors, and VPs, it is quite easy to understand why some groups flourish within a company, and why some struggle. If the leaders of an organization are too buyer-oriented, and always push for more, faster, cheaper, and better, they will eventually burn out their employees and have low employee retention. On the other hand, if the leaders of a company are highly compassionate, understanding, and heavily favor the makers, they will likely have a happy, but totally inefficient, team since the importance of satisfying the buyers and the financers are neglected. If this is the case, then it can and should be the role of sub-managers to compensate, so that within the team, there is a balance of voices. Buddhists often refer to this as the

Middle Way:[34] to balance, not by avoiding extremes, but by balancing them out.

As an efficient manager, ask yourself this question: In my chain of command (this can include the chief executive officer (CEO), the VP, and the director for example), are the interests balanced? If yes, then is this balance perceived by your resources or does one group feel neglected? Are you creating any sort of imbalance? Are parts of your team lacking managerial support regarding one of these three entities that are inhibiting their interests, and limiting your group's success?

A simple table can help you understand these concepts. In the example illustrated in Table 1, unless the manager is willing to put a lot of work into the human resources department or is naturally very human resources-oriented, their team will fail.

Table 1: The 3 corporate entities example

Person in Chain of Command	Percent of Time / Effort thinking of		
	Financers	Buyers	Makers
CEO	20 percent	70 percent (obsessed with market shares)	10 percent
VP	60 percent (obsessed with department cost center, budget respect)	20 percent	20 percent
Director	50 percent (obsessed with pleasing VP)	40 percent (want to shine in front of the executives)	10 percent

---

34 https://www.britannica.com/topic/Middle-Way

The efficient manager will notice the lack of effort put into the makers entity, and consequently, they will adapt, and make their team flourish regardless. And they will be successful, appreciated, and most of all, efficient.

CHAPTER 12

MANAGING IRREPROACHABILITY

THERE IS A SAYING in sports: Offense sells tickets, but defense wins championships. Did the legendary American football coach Paul "Bear" Bryant, who said this, know that this notion has roots in Sun Tzu's *The Art of War*? Perhaps not, but this means that there is something to be learned from this concept for the efficient manager. Let's explore.

Tactical Disposition

Tactical Disposition is the translated title of the fourth chapter of *The Art of War*. The very first sentence goes like this: "The good fighters of old first put themselves beyond the possibility of defeat, and then waited for an opportunity of defeating the enemy."[35]

In a competitive environment, this means securing the defense. Make sure you do not get scored on, and then you cannot lose. Often due to impatience, or wanting to rush,

---

35 Translation from Lionel Giles, Chapter IV, line 1

the other party will eventually expose a weakness, or an unprotected side. Because they are so focused on winning, they do not realize they are engineering their own defeat. For corporations, "securing the defense" may mean securing cash cows, and only then attempting to win other markets, without ever forgetting to take care of the cash cows.

It is much easier to defend a position than to conquer a new one. To attack, we must possess an overabundance of strength, and deploy considerable effort and resources, sometimes only to obtain marginal or non-existent gains, which is something the efficient manager does not like to do. Once the defense is secured, we can now make use of these excess resources to attack when it comes time to seize the opportunity. One must have wisdom to recognize what is worth fighting for and when it is appropriate to push forward.

In managerial situations when competition is not the name of the game (management includes moving a group toward objectives, working with allies and colleagues to achieve greater, faster, and cheaper results), this "playing defense" comes down to one word: irreproachability. This means always securing your current positions, always putting yourself in the shoes of those who look to blame you for failing to execute or report this or that task and making sure they have no arguments to use against you and no opportunities to fault you.

Being irreproachable does not mean blaming others, as this goes against the values of the efficient manager that were discussed in the chapter on self-mastery.[36] It means leaving no loose ends; securing your flanks. Furthermore, never let your guard down and always watch out for what was already acquired. Never take your previous successes for granted, as this opens up the possibility of attack.

In that chapter, I also mentioned that the only being we fully control in this world is ourselves, and consequently, we can only control what we do and our own strategy. If we leave no opening for attack, we cannot lose. Sun Tzu explains this a little further on in Chapter 4: "To secure ourselves against defeat lies in our own hands, but the opportunity of defeating the enemy is provided by the enemy himself."[37] This point brings us back to what was discussed above: due to greed, or because one is power-hungry, impatient, over-confident, or backed by a big title, they may want to gain too much too fast, which in turn leaves the door open for you to defeat them, or at least gain the upper hand. Sun Tzu concludes this section by saying: "Thus on the one hand we have ability to protect ourselves; on the other, a victory that is complete."[38]

The efficient manager must secure their previously captured gains, then wait for an opportunity, a favorable situation, to improve their position. If they try to force the situation, they will put themselves at risk. Opportunities

36 Chapter 10
37 Translation from Lionel Giles, Chapter IV, line 2
38 Translation from Lionel Giles, Chapter IV, line 7

always eventually present themselves. When secure, we can then plan the next move in total safety.

Such is the importance of irreproachability concept that Sun Tzu revisits in Chapter 6: "You can be sure of succeeding in your attacks if you only attack places which are undefended. You can ensure the safety of your defense if you only hold positions that cannot be attacked."[39] Several phrases in *The Art of War* refer to the depletion of resources on one front to reinforce another, which leads to the weakness of the defense as one example of failing to maintain a strong defense and leaving an opening for attack. In a managerial situation, this would translate to leaving you open to potential reproach or blame. Quebec City is one of the only fortified cities never taken, and never invaded once the fortifications were built. The reason for this: it was never attacked. This is the apogee of being irreproachable: leaving others no reason to attack in the first place.

---

39 Translation from Lionel Giles, Chapter VI, line 7

CHAPTER 13

MANAGING PEACE

THE 2020-2022 COVID pandemic forced us to be resilient. If utilized properly, resilience can lead to peace of mind and to mastery of emotions. In a previous chapter,[40] I briefly discussed the importance of self-mastery, including becoming the master of our emotions. I wrote that everything we do is an opportunity to cultivate ourselves and work toward that self-mastery. Let's dive a little deeper into this concept of emotional self-mastery, that has its goal as eventually achieving, or at least approaching Inner Peace. Let's take a look at how to "master" peace.

Defining Peace

Cambridge Dictionary defines peace as "freedom from war and violence, especially when people live and work together happily without disagreements."[41] This is obviously not something one can master on a global scale on their own. For managers and non-managers alike, I like

---

40 Chapter 10
41 https://dictionary.cambridge.org/dictionary/english/peace

this definition of peace (unknown author) that focuses on self-mastery:

Peace, it does not mean to be in a place where there is no noise, trouble, or hard work. It means to be in the midst of those things and still be calm in your heart.

One way to cultivate this personal type of peace (inner peace) is developing resilience.

Life throws at us a lot of unpredictable events to which we may react emotionally or rationally, with joy, surprise, love, anger, jealousy, or sadness. Learning to build resilience when dealing with these unforeseen stressful events, where emotions are likely to come into play, may be challenging, and feel almost impossible. If you are continuously under stress, and fail to willingly practice facing stressful situations, the light will likely never shine at the end of the tunnel. In fact, the tunnel will actually never seem to end.

Knowing this information, in addition to meditation and self-awareness activities, a good practice is to willingly, and purposefully, place yourself in a challenging/stressful situation and practice breathing, and staying calm in face of such adversity. These short but intense stressors are called *hormetic stress* and sublethal exposure to hormetic stress can induce a response that results in overall stress resistance. Exposing yourself to these stressors teaches you to develop your resilience: If you can stay calm, and centered in such situations, then your mind learns that whatever life may throw at you, you'll be okay because you already have the tools to stay calm and at peace. The practice of voluntary discomfort does more than just make us appreciate comfort; it teaches us to have a high tolerance for that which is uncomfortable. It is something we should practice because it gives our mind and body the confidence that, since we have already survived these minor periods of discomfort, we can also survive major discomforts. In simpler words, it is a practice of becoming okay with discomfort.

Simple activities that one can easily add to their routine to trigger hormetic stress are practicing intermittent fasting, cold exposure (daily cold showers for example), or hypoxia (controlled oxygen deprivation via breathwork). In addition to help building resilience, both physical and mental, these activities have several documented health benefits. Documented benefits may include boost your body's functioning and help you build tolerance to greater stresses[42], help prevent or lessen the severity of many conditions, including allergies, autoimmune diseases, and coronary heart disease[43] or in some cases lower risk of neurodegenerative and cardiovascular diseases[44].

Resilience doesn't come hard-wired into us at birth, but, just like a muscle, it's something one can build and grow over time with practice. Our ability to boost our resilience relies primarily on a capacity of the brain known as neuroplasticity, or the ability of neural networks in the brain

42 https://www.google.com/books/edition/Dopamine_Nation/v80AEAAAQBAJ?hl=en&gbpv=1&dq=dopamine+nation+hormesis&pg=PA148&printsec=frontcover
43 https://www.jstage.jst.go.jp/article/jpa2/29/4/29_4_127/_pdf/-char/en
44 https://www.sciencedirect.com/science/article/pii/S0531556521002916?via%3Dihub

to change through growth and reorganization. The mind can still learn and develop well into adulthood. Placing ourselves in a difficult position will cause the neurological processes in the brain to excite with activity. The key is then to calm yourself in this situation. Continue to repeat this process and eventually the mind will learn to automatically stay calm and focused on dire purposeful situations, and more importantly, it will also remain calm in dire unplanned situations. Transformation is slow and gradual, but consistent practice can lead to a complete renewal of oneself.

To quote Wim Hof, the Iceman: "Spontaneous events are puzzles in the mind that you have to figure out on the go. It's a part of living in the present. You have to be ready to mold yourself to whatever life gives you. To be ready, you must be alert within."[45]

Equanimity

Equanimity is a state of mental calmness, composure, and evenness of temper, especially in a difficult situation.[46] The Dalai Lama said: "When our minds are clouded by hatred, selfishness, jealousy, and anger, we lose not only control but also our judgment."[47] One becomes a master of neither

---

45 https://quotefancy.com/quote/2836596/Wim-Hof-Spontaneous-events-are-puzzles-in-the-mind-that-you-have-to-figure-out-on-the-go
46 https://medium.com/@twoguyswhoblog/the-definition-of-equanimity-is-mental-calmness-composure-and-evenness-of-temper-especially-in-4a2a4db383a9#:~:text=Save-,The%20definition%20of%20equanimity%20is%20mental%20calmness%2C%20composure%2C%20and%20evenness,triggers%2C%20perceptions%2C%20and%20sensitivities.
47 Goodreads.com, Dalai Lama XIV Quotes

thoughts nor emotions and consequently, there is a lack of control, and our judgment falters. As managers, we are constantly under pressure to deliver, decide, and cope with strange behaviours, bad news, setbacks, and so on. One must keep a cool head to see the path forward and find a solution that has positive impacts on both the short and long term. There is no place for tantrums, panic, or lack of patience. Every business and every department are better run by a resilient manager: one that stays calm and connected to the situation and their team in times of crisis.

In regard to warfare, Sun Tzu makes a similar point about losing focus, and acting on the decisions made not by reason, but by emotions: "The general, unable to control his irritation, will launch his men to the assault like swarming ants, with the result that one-third of his men are slain, while the town still remains untaken."[48] The hot-headed manager, like to hot-headed general, is likely not in control of their irritation.

What happens to us as managers if we are unable to control our irritation, and if we base our decisions and actions on anger and forget our empathy? A good friend once told me that a good manager should be likeable, but firm when they need to be; you need able to connect well with people, so they want to get things done for you. This can only be done when you find inner peace, and when you see the situation with clear eyes. And the only way to

---

48 Translation from Lionel Giles, Chapter III, line 5

find inner peace? Encountering challenges that build resistance. So go out there and voluntarily seek out discomfort, and one day, you will emerge as a manager who is able to deal with any situation.

How will you challenge yourself today, tomorrow?

CHAPTER 14

MANAGING YOUR NETWORK

THE PHRASE "SCIENTIA POTENTIA EST" is a Latin aphorism meaning knowledge is power.[49] Information can be gathered by two means: you work and dig for it yourself, or it is delivered to you by some source. Your team can obtain information in the same way: they can either work hard to obtain it, or it can be offered effortlessly to them. From the point of view of the efficient manager, which approach sounds best?

Of Roads and Webs

In his very first chapter, Sun Tzu in *The Art of War* talks about the importance of method and discipline and says on the subject: "By method and discipline are to be understood the [...] the maintenance of roads by which supplies may reach the army ..."[50] The manager needs to build such roads all the time to make sure supplies, in this case information and knowledge, travel smoothly and effortlessly

49 https://www.dictionary.com/browse/scientia-est-potentia
50 Translation from Lionel Giles, Chapter I, line 10

between team members and the manager. Information must also flow between the manager and the entire network that could possess data that may be relevant to the manager's objectives.

This efficient manager is essentially building a series of webs, one per finality for example, with links inbetween them. Just like a spider, they do not see everything that goes on in the web, yet, as soon as something does occur, the spider, or the manager, is aware. A bug, a twig, a gust of wind: It may not always be relevant to the spider, but the information is there and available and, finally, explorable if deemed relevant.

Now a manager is more than a spider, of course, and their web should be built in a way that if the information is detected somewhere, not only should they know what the information is, where it comes from, and its relevance (like our eight-legged friend), but that information should (again effortlessly) be carried out and transmitted to other relevant parts of the web without the manager needing to forward it (the manager is not an informant). That way, the entire network is activated whenever pertinent information is available, and the relevant people become aware of this data and can proceed to do what needs to be done. The role of the manager in this case is building the web, making sure it is active and functional, and maintaining it. All the rest is done by the simple presence of the web.

And then when your boss or a colleague tells you that you have a great team that is both responsive and autonomous, what they think they are saying is: You are so lucky to have folks like that to support you. What they are truly saying is: You have built a fantastic network that transmits information with incredible efficiency. And if the web is built correctly, these people should also be part of the web, often without even being aware of it.

Of Allies and Spies

Sun Tzu talks a lot about allies and spies (his entire Chapter 13 is about spies). Before talking more about what they are, let me briefly divide all the manager's contacts and relations into three simple categories:

- First category ("1"): People with whom you have a personal relationship; people whom you can trust, such as friends, confidants, and people who you know will go out of their way to help you.
- Third category ("3"): People who eat up your time and bring no value to your goals; people with whom you may have personal conflicts.
- Second category ("2"): All the others who do not fall into category one or three.

It is much easier to get information to and from a "1" than from a "2", and much easier to obtain knowledge from a "2" than from a "3." So, the more your spider web is composed of "1s", the simpler it is to create, activate, maintain, and exploit.

I would therefore describe an ally as a "1" who is naturally part of the web: your employees, your boss, your contact at various suppliers, your partners, etc. These are the people whom others will understand and find it normal for you to have interactions with.

A spy on the other hand is a "1" who nobody really knows about, who can privately feed you information (through a single isolated spider thread). This person can give you advance knowledge, confidential information, etc. And an ally on one project can be a spy when it comes to other topics.

Now, of course, when some of the threads on the spider web go out to "2s" and "3s", information will not flow naturally, and it will be much harder for the manager to maintain a fluid system. We all know the saying about the weakest link in a chain. In this situation, the manager can work to gather the missing information, or they can put effort into building a stronger relationship with these individuals, which will benefit the manager by hopefully creating an eventual automatic and independent cog in the system. Put in the effort to transform a "2" into a "1." Something else to consider: The effort to transform a "3" into a "1" is probably considerable (sometimes it is not even possible), and that effort is likely larger than the energy required to find a way to remove this "3" from that spot in the web.

This managerial strategy is quite opposed to those managers who want to know it all, control it all, and always be in the action. Do not be operational; be managerial instead. And then sit back, relax, and watch the magic unfold.

CHAPTER 15

MANAGING TIME

TICK-TOCK. A WORKWEEK is 40 hours. That is 2,400 minutes or 144,000 seconds. So much time and so many unique moments, and yet, most of us complain we don't have enough. How can that be? And as managers, how can we achieve more within that ocean of seconds? Tick-tock.

Time as a Resource

After my university years, I was blessed to have the opportunity to do volunteer work in West Africa (Mali) for several months. I learned a lot about human nature, priorities, happiness, and self-appreciation, but one of the most fundamental things I learned during that period was about time. This revelation permanently altered my professional career. Prior to this experience, I was effective, and I always met my deadlines. After this realization about time, which I will share very shortly, in addition to being effective, I started to become efficient. Having been raised in Canada, or more loosely speaking in the occidental-race world, the de facto concept was, and still is, for that matter, that time is a constraint. Here in the West, we always lack time; we are constantly "running out" of it.

My realization was this: time can be seen and should be seen as a resource, not a constraint. And like any resource, it is there at our disposal until we run out of it. So, if time is a resource, it has to be managed properly like any other resource.

We learn to manage money by creating a budget. When we run out of it, we have no more buying power. If we create a budget and don't respect it, we don't achieve our savings goals (for example), and money goes from being a resource to being a constraint. Same thing with fuel: If you run out, the car stops, and so on for any resource. Run out of time, and, well, we die (hence the term deadline), but until that point, time remains a resource, not a constraint.

As long as it is perceived as a constraint, it is normal to not have enough, as such is the nature of a constraint. Once we perceive time as a resource, as something that *allows* us to complete different activities instead of something that *prohibits* us, then we can take control of the time we have, and we can manage it.

Management Categories

In my very first chapter I defined an effective manager as someone who achieves finality by optimizing resources with efficiency. Let's take a look at three different categories of managers in relation to this definition:

1. **The Ineffective Manager:** Someone who has the mandate to achieve objectives and doesn't often do so.

Typically, this person will be great at making excuses and pointing the blame at others. Since their track record is not great, this person will do other things to please their boss and secure their position in the company. This state of mind needs to change completely (for example, they need to start looking at themselves instead of blaming others) in order to proceed to the next kind of manager.

2. **The Effective Manager:** This manager almost always meets their objectives, but quite often when they are questioned on how they are doing, answers will be in the form of I'm always in a rush; I don't have any time left for myself; this was yet another huge week. They do not blame others, but they clearly see time as a constraint that limits them instead of aiding them. This state of mind is the correct one, but they have never learned to visualize time as a resource, and they have never been coached on how to manage it. A manager does not manage constraints; they manage resources, and time is one of them.

3. **The Efficient Manager:** In addition to hitting their objectives, their friends always ask them, "Where do you find the time to do all that?"

Changing the state of mind (the person needs to go from level 1 to level 2) involves deep personal work, and not everybody can do it. Fundamental changes need to occur for the person to stop blaming others or using external circumstances to justify personal failures.

Going from Effective to Efficient, on the other hand, requires a change in perception. This also implies changes in habits. Although this shift does not require the complete alteration of the state of mind, it nevertheless may be difficult for people to put their faith in something they have not experienced. This can require coaching, training, and a willingness to explore other ways of seeing, and doing.

In my experience, when this gap between Effective and Efficient is bridged, 20 percent-30 percent of the workweek can be freed up (often much more using the Pareto Principle described in Chapter 1). But now, the fundamentally effective manager that suddenly sees 20 percent-30 percent potential free time, wanting to be effective, just uses this time to check something else off the to-do list. So, time is never actually freed, it is just consumed by other menial and operational things that they would not have had time to do had they not "freed up" that 20 percent-30 percent. These tasks were therefore likely lower priority and less important. Part of the change in perception is to accept free time and to know that it will be there to relax, ponder, think, question, brainstorm, plan, etc.

And here's something to think about: If a manager cannot properly manage the resource that is time, how can they properly manage other resources? To quote Peter F. Ducker, who according to *Forbes,* is the founder of modern management:[51] "Until we can manage time, we can manage nothing else."[52]

The Pareto Principle – Part 2

So, in Chapter 1, we described how, using the Pareto Principle, or the 80-20 rule, we could spend 20 percent of our 40-hour week, hence eight hours, and get 80 percent of the work achieved, and then 20 percent of the remaining 32 hours, to get 80 percent of the remaining 20 percent work left undone. This sums up to 14.4 hours to achieve close to 96 percent of what really matters and what will impact (as you can see this is much more than freeing "only" 20 percent-30 percent of your time).

We get to this by using the Pareto Principle on the leftover 80 percent. But if we switch things around a bit …

The first iteration of the principle, as mentioned above, gets us 80 percent of the result with 20 percent of the time and effort. But out of that 80 percent of results, some will be more significant. Let's redo the Pareto Principle not on the 20 percent, which is not done as in the first scenario, but on the 80 percent that is achievable. This leads to 20 percent of the initial 20 percent, therefore 4 percent of the total, to accomplish the most impactful result of the initial 80 percent, calculated by 80 percent of the 80 percent, hence 64 percent. So, a little 4 percent of your effort, if

51 https://www.forbes.com/sites/stevedenning/2014/07/29/the-best-of-peter-drucker/?sh=1fd75d75a96e
52 Goodreads.com, Peter F. Drucker Quotes

spent wisely, leads to 64 percent of the overall result and impact following the principle. Then let's do it again … 20 percent of 4 percent will lead to 80 percent of 64 percent … or in other words, 0.8 percent of your effort if done wisely and thought through, can generate 51.6 percent of the impact. Less than 1 percent!

On a 40-hour week, this is around 19 minutes … 19 minutes of your week to achieve more than half of what you will accomplish. This may be a 4-minute email Monday, an 8-minute delegation and explanation Tuesday, a 5-minute reflection that leads to a non-action on Wednesday, an informal 2-minute chat on Thursday…And just like that, you likely have accomplished more than anybody else who is just running down to-do lists. These actions are your top priority, the important ones (important vs. urgent will be explored in Chapter 46) to achieve your goals, and your finality (we will discuss the difference between goal and finality in Chapter 22).

A Few Ideas

Here is a list of ideas to help you transition from lacking time (seeing it as a constraint) to always having enough time (seeing it as a resource).

- Block out "thinking/relaxing" time to find ways to further optimize time usage.
- Look at your agenda of a typical week and see where time is going: Where are the time black holes, the wastes, the possi-

ble optimizations, and track your progress week after week to see your improvements. Stop saying that you don't have time for yourself while continuously spending two hours per day looking at Facebook or Netflix.

- Budget your time. If you don't have a budget before going to the casino, you will come out broke. Allot a certain amount of time for tasks and respect that "budget." If you cannot respect your budget, realize that you are working on borrowed time (time that you allotted to another task) and willingly cut time from that other task, not from the blocked "thinking/relaxing" time. Similarly, budget "contingency time" for unforeseen events.

We are all so caught up on obsessively completing our to-do lists and on "racing time." Seeing time as a resource instead of a constraint allows us to optimize it and get the most value out of it. Let's get back to being "human beings" instead of "human doings."

CHAPTER 16

MANAGING HAPPINESS

HAVE YOU EVER HEARD of the term "Hedonic Treadmill"? What about the expression "Happiness Set Point"? Both expressions actually mean the same thing: They refer to our level of subjective well-being that is determined primarily by heredity traits and personality traits ingrained in our early in life, and as a result, this "happiness set point" remains relatively constant throughout our lives.[53] Let's explore this concept.

Happiness vs. Pleasure and Suffering vs. Pain

Positivepsychology.com defines the Hedonic Treadmill as "a theory positing that people repeatedly return to their baseline level of happiness, regardless of what happens to them."[54] Of course, on a daily, weekly, monthly, and yearly basis we are not at a constant level of happiness. Events happen: happy events, sad events, frustrating ones,

---

53 https://www.psychologytoday.com/ca/blog/happiness-in-world/201304/how-reset-your-happiness-set-point
54 https://positivepsychology.com/hedonic-treadmill

etc. Our mood fluctuates, but this fluctuation produces an average. This average is our happiness set point.

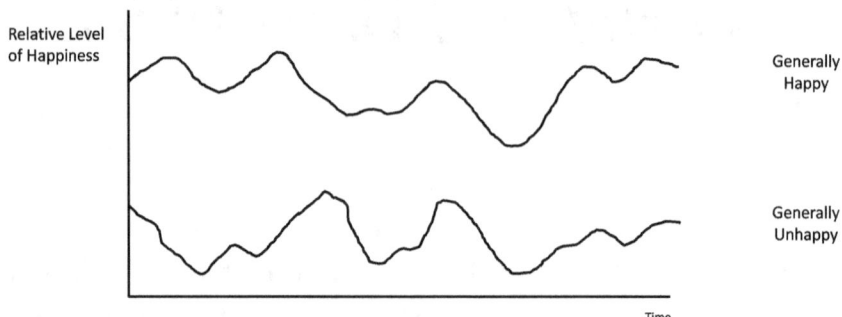

Figure 2: *Example of relative happiness over time*

The higher the relative average, the happier you generally will be.

Peaks on the chart above refer to pleasure, while the overall tendency is happiness. Pleasure is short-lived and usually triggered by an event (for example, pleasure can be triggered by good news, a promotion, an acquisition, or even a certain activity). Happiness, on the other hand, is long-lived and consists of a general state of being. We all have pleasant moments, but these pleasant moments do not necessarily mean we are fundamentally and consistently happy.

Some may even try to periodically retrigger a pleasant moment they have previously experienced, believing this will bring long-term happiness. In fact, this pleasure-seeking behavior often creates dependencies and does not increase the happiness set point.

Similarly, low points on the graph represent pain. No one can avoid pain: We all experience moments of devastating pain (for example, a loved one dying), and moments of negligible pain (we might bump our knee on a piece of furniture). Just like pleasure, pain is short-lived and triggered by an event. Letting this event drag on by reliving it, or by feeling guilt or regret, for example, leads to suffering, which is a much longer state. Suffering, not pain, lowers our happiness set point.

In both cases, notice the difference: We HAVE pain, or we HAVE pleasure. On the other hand, we ARE happy, or we ARE suffering. Short-lived events, triggered by whatever happens in life, causes us to have both positive and negative feelings. These do not define who we are in the long run.

Changing the Hedonic Treadmill

As was mentioned in my chapter Managing Success, The Dalai Lama defines the purpose of life as Finding Happiness. Since pleasure is based on short-lived events and is associated with the verb **to have**, and conversely, happiness is associated with the verb **to be**, it brings us to the question: Which is more important in our lives? To work, struggle, and spend time and effort **to have** as much as possible? Or to work on ourselves in order to grow, to change our state of mind, and **to be** as much as possible? I ended my previous chapter with a proposition: Let's get back to being "human beings" instead of "human doings." Here, I offer a slightly modified version: Let's get back to being "human beings" instead of "human havings." This idea is harmonious with another quote from the Dalai Lama: "We need to learn how to want what we have, NOT to have what we want in order to get steady and stable Happiness."[55]

So, is it possible to change our happiness set point if it refers to traits ingrained in us early in life? Is it really permanently "set"?

Studies such as the one from Springer Link[56] show that the happiness set point remains relatively constant and unchanging unless we radically change our way of being. Interestingly enough, the trait most strongly associated with long-term increases of the happiness set point, according to these same studies, is a commitment to altruism. The more we focus on helping others, and on being compassionate, the happier we become down the road (another study[57] also suggests that altruism causes the increase of the happiness set point).

Is it really a surprise then that the man dubbed as the happiest man alive,[58] the Buddhist monk Matthieu Ricard,[59] writes book after book and makes speech after speech on the importance of altruism? You can listen to

55 Goodreads.com, Dalai Lama XIV Quotes

56 https://link.springer.com/article/10.1007/s11205-009-9559-x

57 http://sonjalyubomirsky.com/wp-content/themes/sonjalyubomirsky/papers/LSS2005.pdf

58 https://www.independent.co.uk/life-style/a-69yearold-monk-who-scientists-call-the-world-s-happiest-man-says-the-secret-to-being-happy-takes-just-15-minutes-a-day-a7869166.html

59 https://www.matthieuricard.org/en/

one of his TED Talks at the link found in the footnote below.[60]

So how do you increase your happiness set point? M. Ricard mentions that altruism is essentially an intention or a motivation. To be altruistic, the ultimate goal of your thoughts, your words, and your actions has to be to benefit others.[61]

If altruism is an intention or a motivation, then it is also, therefore, a choice, and one that we can make every day. As managers, how can we increase the happiness of our teams and build a culture of altruism? Happier teams are more motivated, more mobilized, and generally perform better. As human *beings*, what will you choose to be today?

---

60 https://www.ted.com/talks/matthieu_ricard_how_to_let_altruism_be_your_guide?language=en
61 https://thehoya.com/ricard-discusses-altruism/

CHAPTER 17

MANAGING
THE ULTIMATE EFFICIENCY

EFFECTIVENESS IS DEFINED AS following a plan to achieve a goal. But can there be a different definition that comes from ancient Chinese texts? In a previous chapter about Managing Expectations,[62] I discussed the role of planning versus the role of a plan. Here I will push this concept a bit further by comparing the typical planning approach used in management to the approach depicted in Sun Tzu's *The Art of War* and various other ancient Chinese texts, such as the *Tao Te Ching*[63] from Lao Tzu.[64] The *Tao Te Ching*, as per Britannica, is a Chinese classic text written around 400 BC. It is a fundamental text for both philosophical and religious Taoism. It also strongly influenced other schools of Chinese philosophy and religion, including Legalism, Confucianism, and Chinese Buddhism, which was largely interpreted through the use of Taoist words and concepts when it was originally

---

62 Chapter 3
63 https://www.britannica.com/topic/Tao-te-Ching
64 https://www.britannica.com/biography/Laozi

introduced to China. Its influence has spread widely and it is one of the most translated texts in world literature. Lao Tzu, as such, is the founder of philosophical Taoism, and a deity in religious Taoism and traditional Chinese religions.

Objective vs. Consequence

We typically build a plan based on the objective we wish to achieve. Once the objective is defined, we look for means, actions, and activities to render this objective possible. A plan is therefore born: a sequence of timed and organized operations drafted to achieve the desired goal. There is even an English expression that summarizes this: *A means to an end*. The "means" in this saying is not valued or important in itself, but its purpose derives from its ability to help achieve an aim. On one side of the saying, we have the entirety of the resources available (this encompasses both the tools and the milestones that make up the plan), and on the other side, we have the prize toward which we try to progress.

It is by examining this process that can we define "effectiveness." Effectiveness is the ability to achieve the means that will lead to an eventual goal. The "action" is born from this planning approach: The action is what you use in order to activate a tool or a means.

Regardless of the management structure, this concept is present in one shape or another. Marketing plans, project plans, triennial plans, restructuring plans, and optimization plans all have a list of activities, to-dos, and milestones that aim to complete an objective. And obviously, this type of approach leaves an opening for failure: Between the means and the end, there is always a chance that one or many unpredictable events occur that limit or jeopardize the plan and that put the goal out of reach.

The ancient Chinese texts propose an alternate approach and an alternate definition for effectiveness. In these texts, effectiveness comes not from the application of a previously defined plan, but from an exploitation of the situation as it is. Instead of seeing a goal and backward planning activities to lead to that goal, you must constantly perform a meticulous evaluation of the situation and evaluate how the situation will progress naturally as it currently stands (Tao defines this natural progression as "the Way"). Then, with this information, you use the situation, not a plan, to move towards the objective. Just like a river carries a floating object, one lets themselves be carried by the current of reality. This causes a constant progress toward improving one's situation. The strategy consists of making the situation evolve such as the effect progressively comes to be on its own. The manager builds the effect **as a consequence** of the situation.

To empty a bucket of water, one can have a plan. They have the option to go get a cup, and scoop by scoop, they will hit different milestones: a third empty, half empty, two-thirds empty. If it rains, if they get injured, or if the cup breaks, the plan is disrupted, and the goal will be delayed or simply not achieved. If one instead decides to create a hole at the bottom of the bucket, the bucket will necessarily empty itself eventually, whether it rains or not. The "emptying" is now built into the situation, and it cannot not happen.

Sun Tzu applied this thinking to a much larger scale and wrote, "Thus it is that in war the victorious strategist only seeks battle after the victory has been won, whereas he who is destined to defeat first fights and afterwards looks for victory."[65] The good general knows victory is predetermined since it is implied in the nurtured situation.

In short, instead of trying to create an effect, the manager should make it a natural consequence of the situation. Instead of a Means-End relationship, this approach is a Condition-Consequence relationship.

To Do or Not to Do

Once the conditions are present (either created or noticed in the current way of things), or once the "hole" is created in the above example, the finality becomes unavoidable. So, what action remains then for the general, for the strategist, or for the manager to take? As the finality is unavoidable, anything they do to alter that situation may change the predetermined outcome because an action always intervenes with the flow of things. When the flow

---

65 Translation from Lionel Giles, Chapter IV, line 15

is guaranteed to arrive at the desired outcome, why inter-vene? Therefore, the best action is taking a "non-action" in this case, hence the switch from action to transformation, and from effectiveness to efficiency. Effectiveness, follow-ing this approach does not come from the completion of milestones, but from a constant adaptation to the flow of reality, and to the renewal of the situation.

Because this strategy points to the constant transfor-mation of the situation, nobody notices this new, trans-formed reality: Nobody can point at a specific moment in time or at a specific deed and say that is the moment when things definitively shifted. Similarly, we just realize one day that our nails need to be trimmed, but this does not mean that they suddenly grew overnight: Their growth hap-pened gradually, and it occurred as a natural consequence of being a human with nails. Furthermore, since nobody notices a "natural transformation," nobody opposes it, so the manager, or the general is able to progress effortlessly, and without resistance.

To reiterate, the manager does not need to act to have the consequence occur. It is not the general or the manager that makes things happen, or that acts to create things, but the situation that gradually reaches its natural finality. For example, if you as manager delegate, you must act and impose your will, whereas if you create the conditions to ensure someone does or volunteers for the work, the effort will come from this volunteer and the task will be done more swiftly, smoother, and as part of the natural progression of things. Authority is most complete when it is hidden, when it is not obvious. And in this way, we can navigate constantly and naturally toward achieving our objectives in the most efficient of ways.

The natural transformation replaces the direct action. This means that a non-action serves to support the current progression of things (instead of risking opposing it) so that the desired outcome is eventually reached. **This does not mean being inactive:** The manager must monitor in order to further understand the situation and they must accompany the natural progression. They must remain involved to make sure this natural progression occurs, and that the correct finality comes to fruition. And thus, the barrier between "Do" and "Done" fades away.

The manager should follow the river and be carried by it. The manager that knows the river always ends in the ocean will always achieve their desired result in the end.

This is what the saying "When nothing is done, nothing is left undone" is all about. In can be found in another form in the Tao Te Ching: "A truly good man does nothing, yet nothing is left undone. A foolish man is always doing, yet much remains to be done."[66]

Practical Application

In today's reality, however, one of the downsides of such an approach is that sometimes such transformations may

66 Tao Te Ching, Chapter 38, translation by Stephen Mitchell

be long, and the effect may come after it is required. In this case, action is sometimes needed. But through this action, and through these short-term milestones and results, a longer-term transformation can occur, which mixes the best of the Means-End approach and the Condition-Consequence approach.

Another downside of such a strategy is that nobody notices the impact of the manager or the general. The success is so complete, and the transformation is so gradual that the end appears to arrive naturally, leading it to go unnoticed. Victory seems so obvious, and so easy that no praise is given. For a manager that values efficiency, not receiving praise is in fact the greatest of praise. To again quote Lao Tzu: "The sage does not attempt anything very big, and thus achieves greatness."[67]

---

67 Tao Te Ching, Chapter 63, translation by Stephen Mitchell

CHAPTER 18

COACHING, OR, IN OTHER WORDS, MANAGING

A MANAGER IS SOMEONE who manages human resources, among other things. Teams, employees, partners, and suppliers all must be managed to achieve objectives. The more skilled and efficient those people are as individuals, but also as a team, the better the team will perform both in terms of quality and efficiency. The more the team is skilled, the more the manager can let them be. If the team is efficient, then the manager can let them progress on their own, while only providing small tweaks to sail towards the set goals with confidence and peace of mind.

But how do we make teams that good, and that efficient, both as individuals, and as a team? How do professionals get better, and continuously improve? This is where coaching comes into play.

To Coach Professionals

In a great Ted Talk,[68] Dr. Atul Gawande makes the point that most professionals learn most of what they apply in their jobs during school and during their first few professional years. They also tend to pick up new skills when they change jobs (as they need to "relearn"), but at some stage, most people hit a plateau. This set of achieved skills becomes the way they work, and the way they "are" in the workplace. The exception lies mainly in sports, Gawande argues. Regardless of how good you are, as a team or as an individual, in sports, there is a coach. Lionel Messi, Tom Brady, and Serena Williams all have a coach despite their incredible skill level at their sport.

So, can this fundamental "always able to be coached" principle in sports be applied to professionals in other industries? To members of a manager's team, for example? There is a coach in sports because situations, colleagues, and partners change, and because one can always improve. A coach sees things from a different perspective and can make tons of micro-alignments and improvements on behaviors and reflexes that would otherwise go unnoticed or unchecked. Without this, somewhere down the road, the professional will stop improving and become stagnant in their skillset. Coaching often realigns small things, but quite often, small things matter. Think of the saying,

---

68 https://www.ted.com/talks/atul_gawande_want_to_get_great_at_something_get_a_ coach?language=en#t-989306

"The devil is in the details." That is how we go from good to great to world-class. The coach can see the forest, and the sky, and they can even smell the air, whereas the individual is rooted in place and constantly stuck seeing the same things from the same perspective. The coach can bring a whole new level of awareness. They shed light on a new path.

We all agree that the coaches of the best players in the world were likely not better than them if/when they were players themselves, but they nonetheless see the details that can transform the great into the greatest. Similarly, a manager that coaches managers can teach them to become better managers, and in turn, become better coaches for their own teams. For example, a manager of software developers does not need to be great at software to coach their team: They can instruct them on how to communicate, document, prioritize, and close better and they can help build team spirit and cooperation.

External consultants can certainly help, but they typically have their "recipe," and are not totally familiar with the individual's situation or the manager's goals and vision. The person who is best positioned to observe, help, align, and train the individual and the team in line with specific objectives, is clearly the manager.

Coaching does not mean dictating or delegating, nor does it mean that the individual being coached is incompetent. Learning has no limits: it is a continuum, and there is always something new to be explored.

Coaching helps the individual progress. It refuses stagnancy and instead works to make each person become as great as they can become. And in turn, the coach also progresses, causing them to grow and learn as well. Coaching rejects stagnancy: the more you observe and criticize, and the more you notice areas to improve, the more you will be able to dedicate yourself to the task of self-improvement. Coaching pushes you to develop the habit of refusing to be content in your own complacency and stagnancy. It inculcates a habit of self-questioning, of thinking and of learning on your own, and of constantly challenging the self in order to become better. Through this process, the coached, and the coach, continuously progress.

For the coached, as well as for the coach, the process can at times be painful. It is not always easy to be observed, to critique, or be critiqued. It is also not always obvious to see the small details, explain them, receive them, and then make changes. And sometimes, while trying to implement the changes, things can seem to get worse. This is normal: we are trying new skills, and new approaches that bring us out of our comfort zone, but, in the end, the result is always growth and improvement.

There is a Chinese saying that sums up the importance of coaching pretty well. It says: "If you want one year of prosperity, grow grain. If you want 10 years of prosperity, grow trees. If you want 100 years of prosperity, grow people."

Different Ways to Coach

Depending on the situation, a manager can approach coaching in different ways. A manager can adopt a "Follow-Me" attitude as they lead the charge with great leadership skills (think: Captain America or William Wallace). This provides great opportunities to coach people on good leadership, and the importance of responsibility, through the creation of feedback loops for example.

A manager's role can be at the back of the group, as well as the one supporting the team and making constructive suggestions. This creates an environment of empowerment, and once a team is empowered, coaching opportunities become numerous.

Finally, the manager can work side-by-side with the team. Here the manager is part of a team and is immersed in the situation, where coaching is obviously easy to do.

Whatever role the manager takes, coaching is always a possibility as long as the manager is open to it and is aware of its necessity and its power.

As managers, we are responsible for the learning and development of each individual under our umbrella. This means taking responsibility for our team and making a commitment to coach, mentor, and seeing to the success of each individual and of the team as a whole. Coaching leads to more efficient teams, more altruistic teams, and more open teams. It leads to employees trusting and appreciating their manager, which leads to increased loyalty and an increased desire to grow and become even more. Ultimately, coaching leads to managing more efficiently.

In *The Art of War*, Sun Tzu is quite direct about this concept. In his very first chapter, you can find on lines 13-14 the seven questions you must answer to foresee victory. One of these questions is: "On which side are officers and men more highly trained?" And who has the responsibility to train them if not their general?

Care about your team. Show them the way. They will grow and carry you to success while you grow and carry them to success.

CHAPTER 19

MANAGING EXPERTISE

THERE IS A SAYING that goes like this: "Practice makes perfect." I think that is actually completely false, especially for a manager. Every human interaction is different: Our past experiences and our ability to understand the reality of another can only ever give us a partial understanding of a new situation. Being perfect in an environment that is ever-changing, and only ever partially known is simply impossible.

But, while it cannot make us perfect, practice should make us better. So, the question is: What do we practice? And what should we practice in order to become better?

False Practices

When I initiate people to meditation, a comment that comes up quite often is: "I try, but I cannot focus on my breath, and my mind always drifts away. I get frustrated or discouraged that I will never be able to concentrate on my breathing, and I start to doubt myself."

"Well," I say, "it seems to me you are not practicing meditation, but you are instead practicing frustration and self-doubt."

We become good at what we practice, and this concept applies to what we think about, and what our state of mind looks like. The more we practice certain states of mind, the more they become our "cruise control," or our go-to reaction. Do you worry a lot? The more you worry, the better at it you will become and the more naturally it will come to you. Worrying becomes your unconscious and instinctive state of mind and even without realizing it, over time you will worry more and more.

In your daily management, do you practice impatience, worry, frustration, and high expectations? Or do you practice compassion, problem-solving, altruism, coaching, and growth? Do you practice being in the operational state of mind, being in the action, and going down lists of to-dos? Or do you practice being a manager, a leader, a mentor, or any other kind of person you believe you should be in order to go from good to great?

Do you say to yourself, "I don't coach because I'm not too good at it and I don't have time for it"? If we only do what we can do, we will never be more that what we currently are. Freeing some time or becoming a coach doesn't come on its own, but this is true for becoming better in any way. If the direction we take always leads back to ourselves, we never go anywhere further than where we already are.

This book highlights many ways a manager can grow, learn, and evolve. However, managing and managing well are not binary switches that are flipped once one reads a chapter. The skills are not acquired instantaneously. It starts with a state of mind of humility and of openness. Managers are often promoted from a more operational job (such as engineer). What made you a good engineer is not the same skillset as what will make you a good manager, and one cannot download the "How to Be a Great Manager" file and be done with it.

Becoming Experts

A day has 24 hours, and let's say on average we sleep for eight hours. This leaves us with 16 hours to practice. We can practice motor skills of course, like learning the piano or kung fu, but throughout the day, our brain is constantly processing thoughts and emotions. As mentioned above, if you worry and doubt yourself often, then you will become great at worrying and doubting yourself. In my chapter on Managing Success, I discussed the importance of managing our thoughts: "Every action we make comes from a thought, or an intention, conscious or not (most often unconscious). It, therefore, makes a lot of sense to pay attention to what type of thoughts we are cultivating (or at least trying to cultivate)."

Thoughts lead to habits and habits lead to character, so practice observing your thoughts, and practice cultivating positive ones.

Back to the 16 hours available to us per day: for how many of these hours do we, for example, practice concentration? How long do we spend concentrating on a task, on an issue, on a strategy, or on what one of our employees is saying without distraction? I would tend to say that the vast majority of us spend very little time concentrating. Let's say two to three hours on average. This leaves us with a massive 13 hours per day, seven days a week, during which we are practicing distraction. And then one wonders why we are so good at being easily distracted, or why it can be so hard to concentrate for more than a few minutes. We are experts at being distracted. How can we teach our teams to focus, and how can we coach them to become better at it, if we as managers practice the exact opposite most of the time?

So how do we become better ourselves at concentration? A great way is by practicing it, a few minutes each day, willfully, mindfully. For example, several daily 1-minute micro-meditations,[69] just focusing on our breath, on our hearing. Practice will make you better, will develop that skill which will, slowly, become natural, and applicable elsewhere.

Practice Makes Better

In my chapter on Managing Talent, I stated that people are great at what they love, and that they love what they are

---

69 https://www.gymondo.com/magazin/en/motivation-en/how-to-micro-meditate-in-60-seconds-to-stay-mindful-even-if-youre-too-busy

great at. I also mentioned that we become great at what we practice. Do you want to become great at managing? Then manage instead of doing. Do you want to become great at compassion and altruism? Practice! Do you want to excel at listening, problem solving, strategizing, concentrating, being on time or switching purposefully from one task to another? Practice these things. But if throughout your day you are often stressed, worried, anxious, and impatient, then this is what you will become an expert at. It does not matter what you have become an expert at over the years; what matters is what type of manager you want to become and what we start practicing right now. To quote Lao Tsu: "When I let go of what I am, I become what I might be."[70]

---

70 https://www.brainyquote.com/quotes/lao_tzu_379182

CHAPTER 20

MANAGING DIFFUSION OF RESPONSIBILITY

THERE IS A POWERFUL sentence in Chapter 10 of *The Art of War* that completely applies to today's management: "When the general's orders are not clear and distinct; when there are no fixed duties assigned to officers and men, and the ranks are formed in a slovenly haphazard manner, the result is utter disorganization."[71] I see instances of this disorganization over and over again at various levels of management.

This leads to a concept called the bystander effect or more often, the diffusion of responsibility.

Social Diffusion

To understand what this term is all about, let's first take a look at the definition of "responsibilization." Wiktionary defines it as: "The transfer of responsibility from higher authorities to communities or individuals who are

---

71 Translation from Lionel Giles, Chapter X, line 18

then called on to take an active role in resolving their own problems."[72]

So, from a manager's standpoint, "responsibilizing" your teams and your resources is of crucial importance. You want to give them ownership for example, and you want to delegate (or as we discussed in previous chapters[73], create a situation in which they take responsibility on their own).

Another definition that can help us further understand the term is from the Sage Knowledge webpage[74] responsibilization refers "to the process whereby subjects are rendered individually responsible for a task which previously would have been the duty of another [...] or would not have been recognized as a responsibility at all."

What about the term diffusion of responsibility then? Britannica.com defines it as: "a sociopsychological phenomenon whereby a person is less likely to take responsibility for action or inaction when other bystanders or witnesses are present. Considered a form of attribution, the individual assumes that others either are responsible for taking action or have already done so."[75] In other words, the phenomenon that occurs when no one acts in a group setting because everyone believes someone else

---

72 https://en.wiktionary.org/wiki/responsibilization
73 Chapters 6 and 17
74 https://sk.sagepub.com/reference/the-sage-dictionary-of-policing/n111.xml#:~:text=Definition,as%20a%20responsibility%20at%20all.
75 https://en.wikipedia.org/wiki/Diffusion_of_responsibility

should or will step up and act. Therefore, no one ends up taking responsibility.

Let's take for example that someone is walking on a faraway trail in the woods, and they encounter a second person that clearly needs assistance. This hiker will likely stop, enquire as to what the issue is, and help as best they can. Now let's say that the same hiker walks into a crowded area and encounters the same individual with the same need for assistance. The only thing that changed from the first situation to the second is the social context. Many of us would walk by, assuming help is on the way, or that someone else will find the time and generosity to help the person in need. Alone in the woods, the hiker will act because if they do not, no one else will, but in a crowded area, they simply assume someone else will handle the situation.

Managerial Diffusion

So how does this concept relate to management? Have you ever seen emails or heard verbal directives that start like this:

- We should do …
- We would need …
- Let's do …

Sentences phrased like these clearly mean that the task being discussed is important, and someone probably needs to do it. However, it fails to specify WHO should execute this task. "We" need to do something but who is this "we"?

Another frequently encountered example is very broad demands, such as communications sent to several people at once, with no clear "who does what":

- Team, please provide feedback on...
- Any thoughts anyone?
- Please submit your ideas...

The general unspoken response to this type of communication is something along these lines: "I don't want to do this," "Someone else will complete this task," or simply, "If I speak first then I'm put on the spot and could face judgement or criticism." Don't be surprised if you or one of your team members uses this sort of phrasing and nothing gets done, or no one volunteers for the task. The Wikipedia page mentioned above actually has a section on workplace diffusion of responsibility: "Diffusion of responsibility can be seen in the workplace through the response to mass email when compared to many, individualized emails. When mass emails are sent out, people feel a lack of accountability due to the fact that the emails have not been addressed to them personally. This is a clear example of diffusion of responsibility. Studies have shown that email responses are more helpful and lengthier when personally addressed because of a greater sense of responsibility than compared to a mass email."[76] While this example from Wikipedia revolves around emails, the concept applies to all communications.

Another example: if you delegate to more than one person, such as assigning dual leadership to an initiative, there is a chance that both appointed "leaders" overlap in their work (inefficient), that both go in two different directions (very inefficient) or that both believe the other one will complete certain tasks, which means these tasks are left incomplete (extremely inefficient). Roles must be clearly appointed. This concept is also touched upon in *The Art of War*: "The art of war, then, is governed by five constant factors to be taken into account in one's deliberations, when seeking to determine the conditions obtaining in the field. These are: [...] (5) Method and discipline. By method and discipline are to be understood the marshaling of the army in its proper subdivisions, the graduations of rank among the officers, [...]."[77]

Now that we have a better grasp of what diffusion of responsibility means, let's revisit the quote from *The Art of War* I used to introduce this chapter: "When the general's orders are not clear and distinct; when there are no fixes duties assigned to officers and men, and the ranks are formed in a slovenly haphazard manner, the result is utter disorganization."

---

76 https://www.sciencedirect.com/science/article/abs/pii/S0747563202000079?via%-3Dihub
77 Translation from Lionel Giles, Chapter III, lines 3-4

An efficient manager should be allergic to the types of communication shown in the examples above, as they provide no clear or distinct orders, and no ranks, which means group unity, and group accomplishments are "slovenly haphazard" (messy and lacking organization). How can this not lead to utter disorganization and chaos?

The Solution

Fortunately, the solution to this issue is quite simple: Use names. Be specific and ask this from your team as well. If someone in your team says, "**We should ...**" then ask who is "**We**" and is that "**Who**" aware that they need to do this task? Did this person commit to doing it? Impose "method and discipline" on yourself, your teammates, and your employees. As Sun Tzu says, "Soldiers must be treated in the first instance with humanity but kept under control by means of iron discipline. This is a certain road to victory. If in training soldiers' commands are habitually enforced, the army will be well-disciplined; if not, its discipline will be bad. If a general shows confidence in his men but always insists on his orders being obeyed, the gain will be mutual."[78]

---

78 Translation from Lionel Giles, Chapter IX, lines 43-45

CHAPTER 21

MANAGING LIKE WINNIE THE POOH

YOU MAY BE THINKING: "What? Is this guy serious? Winnie the Pooh?" And yes, I am completely serious. Let's take a look at two quotes from this loveable huggable bear:

- "People say nothing is impossible, but I do nothing every day."[79]
- "Doing nothing often leads to the very best of something."[80]

If you go back to some of my previous chapters, the high efficiency manager is defined as one who achieves their finality with the least possible effort (ideally no effort or "nothing"). The manager does not DO; they MAKE something/someone DO (make people do, make resources do, make money do, make situations do, and so on). They are not in the operational realm, but in the managerial one. As I said in the chapter on Managing the Ultimate Efficiency: "When nothing is done, nothing is left undone." Lao Tzu speaks on this point: "A truly good man does nothing, yet

---

79 Goodreads.com, A.A. Milne Quotes
80 Goodreads.com, A.A. Milne Quotes

nothing is left undone. A foolish man is always doing, yet much remains to be done."[81] Benjamin Hoff[82] even wrote a book titled *The Tao of Pooh,* which links Winnie the Pooh and his philosophy to Taoism.

In both quotes above, Pooh refers to the concept of "nothing." Let's explore this word a bit more and examine its managerial power and applications.

The Power of Nothing

Have you ever tried to add water to a glass that is already full? Or add tasks to an agenda that has no more empty slots? In these examples, the water or tasks just can't fit in. The only way water can get in the glass is if there is room in it (if part of the glass has nothing in it).

This "nothingness" is what leads to the possibility of filling it. When the glass is full, there is no more potential, and no more options. When it is empty, the possibilities and potential are almost infinite. It is by being empty that something can be filled and achieve its full potential.

This is true for a glass of water and for our agenda. But it is true for any situation. If the situation is already complete (every command given, and every detail inked out), there is no room for growth, for spontaneity, for innovation, and for inspiration. There is no room to react and adapt to a changing reality.

---

81 Tao Te Ching, Chapter 38, translation by Stephen Mitchell
82 https://www.benjaminhoffauthor.com/

It is by creating this emptiness that things can achieve their functions, and that they are allowed to grow and evolve. A tree will not grow wider or taller than the box inside which it is contained. Only when there is space and emptiness can the tree expand and become what it was meant to be. When the effect comes, it is always specific (a tree will always become a tree; nothingness will not turn it into something it is not), but emptiness is the generic and generating condition for this effect to be able to come to pass and to flourish.

If there is no room to grow and expand, the effect will be limited. The impact of this effect will not be carried out and propagated as easily. The wind blows stronger in a field or above a lake than it does in a forest: the emptiness creates and amplifies the effect of the wind.

As managers, other than in the agenda we mentioned above, do you leave space for your team to grow and explore? Do you leave space for your projects, and your endeavors to grow and unfold?

To take it a step farther: Leaving space for people and situations to grow is an excellent start, but creating space is even more powerful. People, things, and situations will grow into the spaces that are available to them. By choosing what space to create, how a space is created and when a space is created, the manager is able to dictate, and impose their will, without delegating or giving out orders. Create nothingness, and the situation will naturally grow into it. Create a void, and air will flow in; create a slope and water will follow it. The same principle is true in managerial situations. Explain a situation and stop talking for example. Silence sometimes speaks much louder than words.

Something full is always limited. Emptiness, on the other hand, is endless. By creating and crafting this emptiness, we can influence the flow of reality. So as managers, create the glass, the container, and the situations that leave room for emptiness so that the natural consequence is the filling of these empty vessels. Manage emptiness and the results will propel you towards your goals.

Like Ray Kinsella (played by Kevin Costner) hears in the movie Field of Dreams: "If you build it, they will come."[83] Build the field, and the player will come. Build a glass, and it can now be filled. Build spaces that contain nothing, and whatever is meant to fill the space will naturally come.

Take "Nothing" Personally

We have explored the power of nothing in situations, on groups, and on the people we manage. However, these teachings can also be applied to ourselves and to our inner world. In fact, we should make use of the concept of nothingness on a personal and individual level if we are to manage others properly. For freedom to come, constraints must go. For something to be generated or to occur, it must have the liberty and the space to do so. It is not the

---

83 https://www.encyclopedia.com/media/encyclopedias-almanacs-transcripts-and-maps/field-dreams

other way around: if you work on creating and adding, but you have already reached your limit and there is no more room, then you will stretch yourself too thin. Your glass will overflow, and you will either fail or lose something or multiple things. This not only has consequences for you as a manager, but also for your team. Here are a few examples of ways to create emptiness in your everyday life:

- Create silences to listen and learn from others and your environment instead of talking and filling silences.
- For fluidity to come, blockages must go. This applies to your exterior world, but it also applies to your interior and personal world. Work on letting go of biases and fixed ideas, and allow yourself to be open to new ways of seeing and doing.
- For motivation to come, procrastination must go. For compassion to come, ego must go. For time to come, activities and to-do lists must go. For the managerial domain to open itself to you, the operational one must go. Let the unwanted go to create space for its natural replacement: when you let go of procrastination, motivation steps in to fill the nothingness you have created.

Work on removing things, thus creating space. Nature will fill in the void. Your life is a rope full of knots. By pulling it, the rope stretches, yet the knots become tighter and eventually the rope will snap. Work on removing the knots instead to allow the rope to move freely.

I would like to finish this chapter with a saying by Lao Tzu: "To attain knowledge, add things every day. To attain wisdom, remove things every day."[84]

---

84 Tao Te Ching, Chapter 48, translation by Stephen Mitchell

CHAPTER 22

MANAGING FINALITY

A FINALITY IS SOMETHING final or a condition from which no further changes occur. Companies must strive for finality in order for the company to grow and survive since as opposed to living things, a company is not born knowing one day it will end. A company, unlike human beings, does not have a fixed finality.

This is quite different from objectives and goals, which are targets to be met and surpassed. When an objective has been reached or missed, then new objectives and goals are set. It is forever a race to the next objective. Finality, on the other hand, is ongoing for a company. Finality consists of surviving and thriving.

Why then are so many companies obsessed with goals and objectives, and so little preoccupied with achieving their finality?

Defining Finality

In the very first chapter, I defined a manager as: "A manager is someone that strategically activates resources to achieve their finality with effectiveness and efficiency."

Since this first section, there have been several chapters that have dealt with many of the terms in this definition, and in this chapter, we will tackle the "finality" aspect. Furthermore, since the manager works for a company, I think it is best to start with the company's finality, and then work our way down to what individuals can do to promote this finality.

As mentioned above, finality for a company is global and ongoing: it aims to survive and thrive. In other words, "finality" refers to the direction in which a company needs to go so that it may bloom and prosper. This finality is not the same for all organizations: a state-owned organization, for example, would not have the same aim of surviving and thriving. Let's segregate what makes up a company's finality (what enables a company to survive and thrive) into two main components:

- A company needs to have market shares, and/or sales, and/or profitability, and/or investments to survive the year. This is what we call the viability of a company.
- It must also make sure to follow and be ahead of the market dynamics. This can be done with new innovative offers that will allow the company to have growth in market shares, and/or sales and/or profitability in the coming years. This is what we call the sustainability of a company.

Of course, no company ever reaches the end of these paths (the path of viability and sustainability). There are always more sales to be made, more profits to achieve, and more market shares to gain, and because of this, the finality is always out-of-reach, and it remains a point toward which we strive for and towards which we constantly try to approach. It is a continuum, which differs from a goal or an objective. Goals and objectives are attainable (you are able to reach a certain percentage of profitability for example), and therefore binary. You can ask, "Was this objective achieved?" and receive a clear yes or no answer.

Sun Tzu's *The Art of War* brings up finality at the very beginning of the text. Finality here is the very survival of the state: "It is a matter of life and death, a road either to safety or to ruin. Hence it is a subject of inquiry which can on no account be neglected."[85]

From Corporate to Individual

Each department of a company, from production to marketing to product definition to finance must contribute to these company finalities. They do indeed have their own individual finalities, but these also help the company tend towards its overall finality.

Obviously, some departments are more viability-oriented (production and sales) while others are more sustainability-oriented (research). This department-specific orientation affects how a manager should behave, manage, and orient their resources.

---

85 Translation from Lionel Giles, Chapter I, line 2

Here are a few simple questions to guide you in this process:

- How do the concepts of viability and sustainability apply to your departments? To your job?
- As a [your title], what is your finality? This question can usually be answered with simple clear statements such as (this example is for a product manager):
    - Viability: Deliver the best projects, with minimal cost, effort, and time.
    - Sustainability: Ensure future projects always become shorter, simpler, and cheaper than what is currently being developed.
- What should your contribution be to these two aspects of your finality?
- What about your team? What role should your resources play in these finalities with respect to their titles and job functions? Have you made your expectations clear, and do they know their specific roles in achieving your department's finality?

Once this is understood, managing becomes quite simple. Just make sure that in everything your team does, they know how they are contributing to achieving your department's finalities. If they do, then turn to the other elements of what it is to be a good manager (efficiency and strategy, for example) to continue to improve your management skills. If they don't, then what is the purpose of taking on the task?

The efficient manager must realize that, often, today's sustainability will lead to tomorrow's viability and vice versa. One always feeds and helps out the other. So even if your team answered the above question with a yes, can you do better? Can the action not only address one component, but both? If you are planning for the long term, can some of these things be implemented now? And if you are solving current issues, can these solutions lead or be turned into permanent improvements?

CHAPTER 23

MANAGING VIEWS AND LEVELS

AS A MANAGER, HAVE you ever experienced a time when a perceptive employee has a vision of how to proceed with a certain task or project, yet, despite repeated attempts to coach them and correct them, they never develop the reflex to share these ideas with their teammates? Or, on the other hand, have you encountered an employee who shares too much, too often, to too many people because they feel a certain sense of globality and community?

Ken Wilber[86] formulated the Integral Theory,[87] which attempts to synthesize different models of consciousness into a complete and comprehensive model. In part to support this theory, Wilber also posited a model he calls "Levels of Consciousness."[88] And as managers, understanding such a model can be the key to understanding many mind-boggling mysteries...

---

86 https://integrallife.com/who-is-ken-wilber/
87 https://integrallife.com/who-is-ken-wilber/#integral-theory
88 https://exploringyourmind.com/the-levels-of-consciousness-and-their-colors/

Levels of Consciousness

Quite often, the examples stated in the first paragraph are rooted in our view of the world and our capability to understand the abstract. A famous (and funny) example is the animated character Shrek comparing ogres to onions. Shrek, being able to understand the abstract, could see that both ogres and onions have various layers, whereas Donkey, being unable to grasp Shrek's level of abstraction, only understands that both are stinky and make people cry.

The more you are self-aware and able to access various levels of abstraction beyond what meets the eye, the higher your level of consciousness. The level of consciousness can be seen as a person's ability to see a multiplicity of perspectives (beyond their own), and this determines how broadly a person can view the world. As these levels progress, you take on a view that encompasses a larger space and a longer time horizon.

And like many models, these levels can be divided into two or three or even ten thousand sections, depending on the level of detail and the granularity of the model. For example, you can divide the different stages water passes through when it goes from freezing to boiling into more or less sections, depending on the level of detail you wish to incorporate. This is further complexified by the choice to measure the temperature in Celsius or Fahrenheit, as both allow for a different granularity. One of the most common models of consciousness in current usage is Ken Wilber's, and this model normally includes 12 stages (with most of the population fitting into five of these levels). In his model, each stage of consciousness is identified with a color for easy reference. It is important to recognize that these "stages" are not strict and distinct levels like rungs on a ladder. They are more like loosely delineated areas along a spectrum.

These are the five levels into which most of the population fall:[89]

- **Red**: Reds are all about, "me, myself, and I" and their way of proceeding is **My Way or No Way**. These individuals are in their default survival mode and their thinking is very much centered around themselves. They make up around 20 percent of the population.
- **Amber**: Ambers prioritize the group or the nation and they tend to value rules, traditional roles, and discipline. For these individuals, the way of their group is **The One Right Way**. Ambers are about 40 percent of the population.
- **Orange**: Oranges value rationality, individualism, and science and are thus able to access many groups and see the possibilities across them in order to seek out the best options. They look for **The Most Successful Way**. Around 30 percent of the population consists of Oranges.
- **Green**: For Greens, everything is contextual, situational, and relative and they view the world as being in constant

---

89 These ratios are from Integral Coaching Canada, Professional Coaching binder (Tab 11, p.16)

MEMOIRS OF A ZEN MANAGER

motion. They see ripple effects and are able to understand the impacts of different actions through time and space. Greens are no longer only focused on themselves as everything is interrelated. For these individuals, **All Ways Are Equal**. These individuals have a global ecosystem view that extends beyond their team and their company, and they make up around 10 percent of the population.

- **Teal**: Teals manage to see a multitude of perspectives and they can perceive systems of systems. They have a multi-dimensional view of the world. These individuals generally uphold **The Best Way for Now**. Teals have a very holistic and world-centric way of perceiving things, but they can also see and understand individuals, teams, and discrete ecosystems. They are about 1 percent of the population.

Note that these consciousness levels are not directly linked to any performance issues, per se.

Each level of consciousness presents recognizable features and a markedly different understanding of the world.

Managing with Colors

So, all these levels of consciousness have colors associated with them. So what? Well, for all colors other than Teal, the individual believes that their view is the right one. That is, they think about where they are, how they live, and what they think is the correct way to "be" in the world. Their entire belief system is specific and incomprehensible to one who does not share their views. Consequently, if you are attempting to have a deep discussion with a colleague, employee, or partner (on a nonoperational level) and you are on two different levels of consciousness, there is a good chance that no clear understanding will be achieved between the two of you, as each interprets what is being said through their own particular level of consciousness.

Since each level believes their view is the right view, a lot of managers may be tempted to force their level onto their employees. For example, if the manager is Red, they might want to lower the level of discussion to the individual (me), and to the present moment (now) or if the manager is Green, they might want to stick to talking about complex multidimensional concepts. The efficient manager, however, realizes this and is aware that not everyone operates on the same level of consciousness. They know their own level and they know their colleagues' levels (either by using such a model or just instinctively).

The efficient manager, therefore, adapts to the level of the person they are interacting with. Even in larger meetings, they can talk to person A in a certain way and shift their style when talking to person B in order to adapt to their level. Remember, levels of consciousness refer to the depth and breadth of what we are able to see when interpreting the information around us and the way in which we relate to what we see. It affects how many levels of interpretation there is for what is available, and what type of abstractions are possible for us at any given moment in time. If the manager talks and acts in ways not accessible to their team, there will be a clear lack of efficiency. For example, talking to a Red can include very concrete sentences, objectives, and things in the "material" world. Avoid talking about impacts on emotions. Agree as much as possible with their views, and tweak accordingly. The focus is on them and the concrete. On the other hand, for example, an Orange may be more triggered by accomplishments, better use of resources, and being more solution oriented. And for a Green, talk about the global objectives, the vision, and the view driving it ... you can leave the concrete world and open up images, and perspectives, including feelings and states of being versus only doing.

This is also true for personal growth books, management books, and blogs. The author writes with the words, concepts, and views of their level. The work will be loved by those at and around the author's level, however, people at a lower level will not grasp the subtlety of the concepts, and people at a higher level will see the material as simplistic, underwhelming, and boring.

Don't Pull on the Plant

As we grow and develop as humans, and as managers, we have the potential to keep growing and to keep expanding our level of consciousness. Yet, because our level of consciousness is the backbone of how we view the world, and because it very much depends on how we live our life and the practices we engage in, it can only shift very slowly. You don't grow two colors by listening to a TED Talk or by reading a book on meditation. As we grow into new levels of consciousness, we start here view our current level with new eyes and we begin to realize that there are some gaps in our perspective, and therefore we explore (on our own or with a coach) until we start to have access to something else, something larger than what we could grasp previously.

Since it is such a long process to even simply work on ourselves, if you try to "force" this process on our colleagues, while over a lot of time (and openness from others) you may see a hint of progress, if the other person is not willingly engaged in such a growth process, then their view will remain what it already is, no matter how hard you try. In this case, you need to adapt instead expecting your team and your resources to meet you at your level of consciousness. Pulling on the stem will not make a flower grow faster. Go to the plant's level and properly nourish it, give it the tools that it needs so that slowly it will grow.

Of course, this color scheme is only a model, meaning it is not perfect, nor does it always accurately describe the reality. You may like it, or you may not. The point is not to sell you the benefits of this model in particular (although I do find this model to be quite insightful) but to illustrate the idea that speech needs to be adapted to the level of the person the manager needs to incentivize and spur to action.

CHAPTER 24

MANAGING IGNORANCE

IN THE CHAPTER "Managing like Winnie the Pooh," I explored the powers of nothingness, or letting the action and the situation unfold to its highest potential. I would like to push that concept a bit further by introducing purposeful ignorance.

I know, you will tell me that knowledge is power, and I do have a chapter about that called Managing your Network. Of course, ignorance is not a manager's virtue. But ignorance on purpose, or pretended ignorance, like Winnie's nothingness, can be a powerful ally.

Pretending We Don't Know

Naturally, the opposite of purposeful ignorance is pretending to know it all. This view can negatively serve us, by making us believe the more we think we know, the less we are open to listening and learning. This leads to presumptuousness, pretentiousness, or simply liking to spread out our knowledge.

As seen in the Dalai Lama, "When you talk, you are only repeating what you already know. But if you listen, you may learn something new.[90]" This demonstrates the idea that purposeful ignorance is the power of pretending to not know.

Once your finality is known, once you understand the concepts discussed in previous chapters about utilizing the potential of the situation, then this method can be a powerful tool. Let's say for example that a colleague, partner, supplier, or client asks us a question. Here are three possible paths:

- We know the answer and we give it.
- We don't know it, we feel a bit embarrassed, and we want to recover by finding the answer to give.
- We know the answer but pretend not to know…

Now why on earth would one pretend not to know? This opens so many possibilities; it's a goldmine of knowledge and potential to be harvested.

We can now ask "stupid" questions to pretend to want to understand. The answers since we know what they are, can easily help us either to steer the conversation or to understand the depth of understanding of our interlocutor. It allows us to learn more about him and his desired outcomes. Specifically:

---

90 Goodreads.com, Dalai Lama XIV Quotes

- It shows we value the other person's knowledge and inputs, putting him in a position of openness or help, and this can be leveraged.
- It gives us the chance to use this "lack of information" to go ask an expert on the matter for his advice. Hence once again we pretend ignorance with that person to open more possibilities in the situation.
- It makes sure we will have a future point of contact with the person who asked the question to provide a future answer. It demonstrates our good faith and our dependability, which again puts coins in the bank for future opportunities.

Don't forget, void creates a natural response to be filled. Pretending not to know, on purpose, opens us to knowledge which would have been hard to obtain with the standard way of responding; since we decide what we pretend to know or not, we decide the path and the knowledge. We create the void to trigger the filling we desire.

About Deception

Sun Tzu in *The Art of War* states that "all warfare is based on deception.[91]" As discussed in the past, working with colleagues, partners, and suppliers is not warfare. They are not the enemies to beat. Therefore, deception is more often not the recommended path. Needless to say, I am not suggesting lying to our colleagues. However, to a question

---

91 Translation from Lionel Giles, Chapter I, line 18

such as "Do you know this?" without using no, an elegant answer would be, "I believe I do, but let me verify before I mislead you...Why do you want to know, how urgent is it, etc." Another example would be the need for certain information from a certain colleague, but you know it might be difficult or appear out of place to outright ask him. It is easier to question him about something else, something you don't really care about or even already know; you are aware that doing so will valorize him and put him in a positive mood. Once the conversation is engaged, it is only a matter of steering the conversation and leading him to where you want to go. As Sun Tzu says: "Rouse him and learn the principle of his activity or inactivity.[92]"

Purposeful ignorance is an excellent opportunity to enhance the other person, but also to enhance your understanding of him and of the situation. It invites one to go directly to his area of expertise or predilection, and since he believes he is leading the conversation, he can have his defenses down.

As an old Chinese treatise on rhetoric suggests (paraphrasing from Guiguzi[93], Jullien[94]):

"According to his knowledge, I certify as true, according to what he says, I highlight the essential, etc. The other therefore evolves in a permanent agreement and recomforting state that gradually

---

92 Translation from Lionel Giles, Chapter VI, line 23
93 http://www.chinaknowledge.de/Literature/Daoists/guiguzi.html
94 https://www.goodreads.com/book/show/330323.A_Treatise_on_ Efficacy

removes his power and allows me to guide the conversation, naturally. By letting myself continuously flow through the situation, I gradually increase my depth of it. The strategy is therefore continuously renewed and endless. In such cases, speech does not serve to talk, but to get the other one to talk, so that I can learn. It allows me to constantly adapt myself to him, to be consequently well received and well believed. I talk to make him speak. I listen to create emptiness in the conversation, thus steering it. It is by adapting myself to his disposition that I can manage him. I follow him to understand him, to lead him. This grip I gradually take over the other is not a result of any hard work, any effort, any forcing, any luck nor magic, but only by always taking advantage of the continuously ongoing flow and process."

All of this is by pretending not to know any better, by working with nothingness. Thanks, Winnie.

CHAPTER 25

MANAGING TERMINOLOGIES

IN A PREVIOUS CHAPTER,[95] I made the subtle difference between a role and a function. To recapitulate: "A manager's function is to achieve a certain result. His role should be defined by the circumstances."

So, what is a role and a function, and how do we differentiate various functions in the management ecosystem?

To Do vs. to Be

To put it simply, a function is what you are paid to do, whereas a role is how you do it. A role is a socially accepted behavior on how to achieve and attend to your function.

Two lawyers in a firm, or two engineers, or two sales representatives will have the exact same function, or to put differently the same job description. Yet how will they each play it out, what role do they have in the movie: authority or agility, direct or subtle, linear or strategic, solo or network builder?

---

95 Chapter 6

- A function is what your job is, what they are paying you to accomplish. For example, a manager is paid to manage, to achieve results with the resources they have available, ideally with minimal effort, waste, and time.
- A role is how you do your job or, in larger terms, how you achieve that result.

Now here comes the previous comment. A manager's function is to achieve a certain result. His role should be defined by the circumstances. Those circumstances include several resources with unique skills and talents: the sociological, political, or economic situation. The function remains the same, yet the situations, circumstances, and conditions are ever-changing, so the role is never the same. The role adapts to reality.

The more operational the job is, the less important the role is. A night janitor or assembly worker has less impact on how they perform their job. Contrarily, the more managerial the job is, or non-operational, the role often becomes more important than the function itself. A manager or director's success is based on their behavior, strategies, and approach, not the title and its function.

In this optic, the often-quoted "Role and Responsibility" matrix does not really make any sense. Terms are important.

Speaking of Terms – Manager vs. Director

I've been asked a few times what my thoughts are, from a managerial point of view, on the difference between the function and the role of a manager and a director.

On the hierarchy scale, let's simplify to have a common base for this discussion:

- The executors, people who accomplish the job, are often divided into groups by expertise and task.
- These groups are managed by a group manager, often task specific.
- Several managers report to a director, often function-specific.
- Several directors report to a VP, often department specific. VPs are also called executives and chiefs.

The executors execute, so it is very much an operational job. Meanwhile, the executives define visions, strategies, roadmaps, etc. It is very much managerial work and non-operational. Those two layers seem straightforward from a definitional standpoint. Pointedly, an executive involved in the operational work is an issue, but it will be addressed below.

What about the middle management then, or the function and role of the director versus that of a group manager?

- The director gives directions. So, their function is to relay the strategies and the visions of the executives to the managers since normally they are not in direct authority over the executors. Most importantly they inform the executives what happens on the operational levels so that the strategies and visions take that into consideration.

○ **They need to make sure to bring the operations into the strategies.**

• The manager manages. They relay "field reality" to the directors since normally they are the ones in direct authority over the executors. But foremost they define strategies to deploy the corporate strategy and vision in the most effective and efficient way, utilizing their resources, the executors.

○ **They need to make sure to bring the strategy into the operations.**

Communication between these layers is paramount, but their roles are totally different. Still, if the director does not get too involved in the operational deployment of the strategy and the manager in the strategic direction, there will be real efficiency across the function. One big issue about this is that a lot of directors used to be managers and enjoy being in the operational. These directors are then promoted to VP and chaos ensues on the organization.

Another Term Misuse

Leadership and management are quite often associated, saying that a good manager is a good leader. Truth is a manager manages whereas a leader leads.

One can be a great leader and lead his army to doom since everybody follows blindly. They have great leadership skills, but no strategic view or efficiency, they just lead. So, a great leader is not by default a great manager. In time, one can be a great manager and always achieve their finality with ease with fewer resources. However, they do all that by pulling strings in the background, networking, and more, with very little leadership skills. A great manager does not by default have great leadership skills.

If the manager has great leadership, then this is just an extra tool in their toolbox they can use whenever the situation calls for it. Nothing more, nothing less. If they don't have this tool, then they will adapt their role, regardless of how they behave to achieve finality.

CHAPTER 26

MANAGING CHANGE

I WAS RECENTLY IN training about "change manage-ment," which introduced the notion of the importance of managers understanding the impact that change may have in the workplace. Change is disruptive, causes disor-der, requires energy, creates systemic negative effects, is a source of stress...Such a negative connotation. Compare this to what Rafiki tells Simba in *The Lion King*: "Change is good."[96]

But for the efficient manager, is change good, bad, or something else altogether?

The Rock and the River

From my past chapter on water and the potential of the situation, let's view change from two perspectives:

- The river: It never knows where it is going or what will come next and yet by being forever adaptive, it always progresses and reaches its destination. Rapids? Falls? Larger banks and

---

96 https://news.disney.com/10-wise-rafiki-quotes-you-need-to-read#:~:text=%E2%80%9C-Change%20is%20good.%E2%80%9D,Embrace%20challenges!

lesser currents? It constantly transforms itself and reinvents itself. It's agile.

- The rock: The rock in the river is strong, solid, confident, stable. It is proud to be a landmark until a flash flood can suddenly make it tip, roll a bit, completely and unexpectedly change the landscape, crush trees, and settle in a new normal.

The rock has had a binary change. The river is a continuous transformation. One is proud of its stability while the other one embraces constant renewal.

So, from the perspective of the rock, change is indeed disruptive. It requires energy and can create systemic negative effects, such as stress. An efficient manager is not a rock.

Power of Daily Changes

Change happens daily. Bad news, a setback, a departure, or a delay are all potential negative changes. A breakthrough, good news, success, or money inflow are some examples of potentially positive changes. But these small changes are often seen as "normal life" until a larger change comes.

Whereas if we learn to see these changes as what they are, constant, constant, constant adaptations, then the entire organization is always in a state of change. People just don't realize it anymore, that change is the unifying agent, the underlying backtrack. Change and adaptation can become the corporate and the individual, depending on the mindset.

Once one realizes that there is this daily motion, daily change, then a world of possibilities opens up:

- Think kinetic energy; it's always easier to steer, accelerate, or slow something that moves than the same object being motionless. Small changes lead to huge transformations that go totally unnoticed.
- If we are always ready for change, we will never be surprised by it. We never need to prepare ourselves for an incoming impact. Water doesn't care if you throw a rock in it, it adapts and continues.
- Even moving at constant speed, changing at a constant rate can be seen as "stable." Therefore, the efficient manager varies this as well. If things go fast, slow them down. If you're feeling bad, then rejoice. If you're feeling too high, then bring it back to earth. Create change so that your team constantly adapts without them noticing their need to adapt.

The power of transformation versus change is:

- Change is binary. We make a change, sometimes radical and destabilizing since it removes the comfort of the current state. When Rafiki says to Simba that change is good, Simba responds, "Yeah, but it's not easy." Simba needed to change from a sloth-like, bug-eating, easy-going, no-responsibility lion to the king of the pride. Binary step function.

- Transformation is a continuum. When you accept this, there is no beginning. When you follow it, there is no end.

Embracing the Change

Instead of fearing change, the efficient manager embraces it. He looks for and creates change, so subtly and often that things evolve, and nobody notices change anymore. Sun Tzu quotes in *The Art of War*: "The four seasons make way for each other in turn. There are short days and long; the moon has its periods of waning and waxing."[97] This may seem obvious, but it just means that things are changing, always. Buddhism talks about impermanence, or Stephen King[98] named one of his short stories collection, *Everything's Eventual*.[99]

In short, the only constant is change. So why not use it to our advantage instead of dreading it? In terms of our daily perspective and actions, this means creating a shift from controlling to adapting, or from controlling the waves to riding the waves.

Consequently, if change is the only constant, everybody, across the organization, needs to develop this state of mind. The more one does this, the more adaptable the organization becomes. In this sense, everybody in the organization is a vector of transformation, and everybody

---

97 Translation from Lionel Giles, Chapter VI, line 34
98 https://stephenking.com/the-author/
99 https://stephenking.com/works/collection/everythings-eventual.html

can be called a manager of change. This is regardless of if you are managing 500 people or just your own schedule and workspace. If you are managing resources, follow and accompany your teams along this path. Trust them, and yet verify that the change, the kinetic energy, and the motion are in the proper direction. Empower and embody transformation.

People have their habits, otherwise known as their comfort zones. It is natural to resist change in that situation. However, transformation is progressive, constant, and unnoticed. So, who can resist and oppose something that goes unnoticed? Trying to "manage change" may be ignoring the potential of continuous transformation, which brings a continuous renewal of the situation and its potential. I call that "The Art of Transformation."

CHAPTER 27

MANAGING
THE ENEMY WITHIN

A CRITICAL SENTENCE IN Sun Tzu's *The Art of War* is: "If you know the enemy and know yourself, you need not fear the result of a hundred battles."[100]

In war, the enemy is often quite obvious. For managers though, we have allies, resources, colleagues, and superiors, but very seldom enemies per say. Still the enemy often lies within; our fears, our doubts, our hesitations, our biases, whatever limits and restrains us. They're the little devils on our shoulder. The Shaolin monks call these internal enemies "mental hindrances," and they define five of them. Learning to identify them and master them enables powerful managerial capabilities.

A way to achieve this mental self-mastery is to go beyond these hindrances, this mental prison or barriers that keep us where we are and prevent us from growing, is to go beyond these hindrances. They are the lines in the sand we draw for ourselves, consciously or not.

---

100 Translation from Lionel Giles, Chapter X, line 31

What are those five hindrances, and how do they play a role in the life of an efficient manager? All of them come and go and take different forms and shapes depending on our journey. So, becoming intimate with them can be a fruitful process.

1 - Sensual Desire

This first hindrance refers to the quest for pleasure and immediate gratification coming from our different senses. (To understand the differences between pleasure and happiness, refer to my chapter on Managing Happiness.[101]) When this need or desire for gratification and pleasure is in control, then our managerial mind is not. The person who wants to lose weight but has a love for food greater than the mastery of his willpower will never achieve his objective. Sensual desires lead to addictions, the desire to always acquire more, or often in the case of managers the need for recognition, to be told "good job" or "thank you." To win the awards, take credit for himself, put his objectives above those of the team or the corporation, and so on.

This can lead to showing off to make sure we are recognized, or to have the hero's role, which directly opposes the argument of total praise in Chapter 17. One can lose his focus and his aim, only by doing things just because they feel good.

---

101 Chapter 16

Someone who is always looking for praise, recognition, and instant gratification may often unconsciously do this to overcome insecurity or to help them go up the ladder. They position themselves as better and different, saying, "Look at me I did this" or "That happened because of my intervention." This happens while internally satisfying the sensual desire need, and this may lead to isolation of the manager. From the words of the Dalai Lama, he mentions that if he sees himself as the Dalai Lama, he is alone, since there is only one. If he sees himself as a normal human being, then he has eight billion brothers and sisters. Looking for praise or seeing ourselves as different creates an isolated prison and removes the manager from the flow. Since his purpose now becomes self-sufficiency, it pulls him away from achieving the objective, the goal, and the finality.

2 - Ill Will and Aversion

Is there anybody in your organization, in your path to achieving your objective, whom you do not fancy or do not appreciate? As a result, you avoid that person, or think "Not him on my team again ..." or simply put up mental defenses and attack stratagems to prepare for the encounter. This is ill will and aversion toward people. But it can also be toward situations that may be unpleasant, like places, moments.... Ill will and aversion make you avoid some situations, willingly or not. Some refer to this as experimental avoidance.[102] But the path to your objective may sometimes go through such people or situations. Avoidance is not an efficient manager's way, as seen in several of the chapters so far.

Ill will and aversion are often based on previous and similar situations or encounters. Trusting that the present and future will be exactly like the past or worse, easily corrupts our ability to judge fairly. This also includes ill will toward oneself, otherwise known as guilt.

Your attitude as a manager is part of the present and will be part of the future. Going to meet these situations with an open heart, an open mind, and some compassion will make the objective in mind remove a lot of that aversion.

3 - Dullness and Heaviness

It's the lack of energy and the lack of motivation. When neither the mind nor the body feel up to the task, we mentally put on shackles. We decide our own motivation, so we decide if we roll up our sleeves and get moving. If we need external motivation, then we go back to the sensual desire hindrance.

The project seems too large? Timeline is unrealistic? Some employees aren't responding or producing? There are many reasons why a manager can feel discouraged by the magnitude of the task. Motivation comes from within,

---

102 https://www.verywellmind.com/experiential-avoidance-2797358#:~:text=Experiential%20avoidance%20is%20an%20attempt,in%20contact%20with%20internal%20experiences.

either by doing things step by step, with smaller steps to make the mountain appear reachable, or by finding a different approach and strategy.

The point is that we decide our level of motivation. It is a state of mind over which we have full control. Like Nike says, "Just do it."[103]

4 - Restlessness

This hindrance refers to the mind shifting constantly. As described in Chapter 19, we are experts in being continuously distracted. When the mind is focused on a task, it is much easier to achieve and to find the solution than when the mind is monkeying around. This is true for the mind, as well as true for a team that has a change in direction and mandates on a regular basis. Calming the mind will calm the team and keep the objective, the finality, in focus. Then, paths and solutions will present themselves.

Just like Master Oogway states in *Kung Fu Panda*, *"Your mind is like this water, my friend. When it is agitated, it becomes difficult to see. But if you allow it to settle, the answer becomes clear."*[104]

5 - Doubts and Scepticism

Having doubts about your actions, your decisions, and your path can often lead to reasons to never perform the

---

103 https://www.creativereview.co.uk/just-do-it-slogan/
104 Goodreads.com, Kung Fu Panda Quotes

action and make the right decision. To worry is to create suffering for something that may very well never occur. As self-mastery explorers, we must realize that the only thing we truly control is ourselves, not the external world. How the world will respond is totally out of our control, so what do we gain in worrying? We can plan to optimize the potential outcome, but at the end of the day we must trust and believe in what we do. If we don't, we will find tons of reasons to not do it.

Wrapping Up

Those are the five hindrances. They are beautifully exposed in Shi Heng Yi's TED Talk.[105] If you want to grow as a manager to an efficient manager, explore how these hindrances are appearing and revealing themselves. See if you want to truly tackle that enemy.

---

105 https://www.ted.com/talks/shi_heng_yi_master_shi_heng_yi_5_hindrances_to_self_mastery?language=en

CHAPTER 28

MANAGING EGO

AS PER THE DALAI LAMA, ego is the number one enemy of compassion.[106] We have talked about compassion quite a lot in the few previous chapters but mainly in Managing Self-Mastery.[107] I would like to dive a bit deeper into the concept of ego and humility, from a manager's point of view, of course.

Manager's Ego

Have you ever met an executive that openly admits to mistakes and openly feeds on the ideas and suggestions of his underlings? Yes of course, but I would argue that this is not the norm. Most believe that they know, that they have the vision, the strategy, and the solutions. They are executives after all. Let's go down a few steps in the hierarchy to middle management, a newly promoted person who became a people's manager for the first time. While some will be humbled by this, many will feel that they are gaining power and authority. They will then start to dictate,

106 https://www.azquotes.com/author/8418-Dalai_Lama/tag/ego
107 Chapter 10

delegate, and protect their turf and their team. They try to show around that they are the boss now. Poor kid. In both cases, at the extreme ends of the managerial spectrum, egos act.

This is in all likelihood a normal process. To be nominated at either of those positions, by a board of executives or an immediate superior, somebody told this person that they were the best for the job, they were great and awesome, and they were the chosen one. Someone that has power and influence did their very best to brush the nominee's ego and make him shine. Now, they want to live up to these expectations towards the superiors, but also show peers and subordinates that the choice was the right one. They establish new rules and new boundaries. Where is humility in such a scenario?

After the pattern is set in motion, they think, well, if this high-ego attitude served me well to get this far, why should I change? Why should I invite humility into my life?

Nevertheless, we demonstrated in various other chapters that compassion is a great tool for efficient management, so ego by de facto becomes the top public enemy. As managers, reflect on your behavior and avoid this ego-centric spiral.

The Field of Humility

A strong ego leads to wanting to dictate, decide, and give orders. It leads to wanting to show strength, since for those people, a manager cannot appear weak and ignorant (refer to my chapter on Nothingness[108] to argue this last point). To decide and impose means being oblivious to the natural evolution, the current reality, and situation. It means one believes his will is stronger than reality. The high ego wants to do, succeed, solve, and shine. In doubt, the high ego reacts first at the moment and emotionally, instead of being rational and considering the global situation.

Yet a manager's efficiency, the ultimate efficiency, is quite elsewhere.

Imagine an uncared and untended field, with a variety of random wildflowers growing in it. In the winter this field seems dead, with brown soil and white snow and ice. It appears to be empty of any form of life. Yet in spring, a transformation starts. All kinds of wildflowers start to bloom and show their magnificence. Each species and each individual flower has its uniqueness in size, color, shape, and potential. What appeared to be empty of life might contain in its oneness the seeds and roots of all different things. Like a manager taking a group, a project, or resources, they have many seeds of greatness. But they need to make them blossom each in their individual way.

In addition, the work of the field does not stop by the end of spring. Throughout the summer, it will care and nourish each individual, supplying them with water, vitamins, and nutrients to help them develop to their fullest potential. The soil does so without discrimination and takes no

---

108 Chapter 24

credit for it. Nobody stops, looks at the field to say, "What fantastic soil!" The soil is always in the background. It accomplishes all of this without taking any actions. The soil never actively does anything. All that happens on its own and naturally. Or put in different words, the soil does nothing, yet nothing is left undone. The soil is all about humility.

The ideal manager, the humble manager, manages like the soil. All resources, projects, allies, and partners, grow to maturity, to happiness, to fulfilment, and to their maximum potential. Yet the humble manager takes no credit for that. Similar to what is said in the *Tao Te Ching* from Lao Tzu, Chapter 17, about the ruler: "He completes his tasks and finishes his affairs, yet the common people say 'these things all happened by nature.'"

If you compare it to the ego-filled field that wants everybody to see how great it is in all its might. Not much grows in such a place. It resembles more of a dead field or a desert! This reminds me of a quote I once heard: "From humility comes responsible leadership. Today, men have rejected humility in order to be first. This is the road to death."[109]

Authoritarian Bullies

A large ego is one thing. An overly large ego is a step more. Especially in the corporate world, we may face

---

109 Author Unknown

people who are power hungry and/or backed by a big title, which makes them believe they can openly be impatient, overconfident, or straight-up bullies. They try to use this power and title to attack, impose, and even intimidate.

Chances are that some people like this are or will be in the organization since often power comes with arrogance, and new leaders will eventually come in to seize power. This is a well-documented phenomena called "self-referential processing,"[110] or being obsessed with oneself. When combined with power and authority, this may lead to "workplace bullying."[111]

Because they have a bigger title, they believe this entitles them to yell, insult, and condemn. They lower others to make them believe they are so much better than them, whereas the truth is we become great by lifting others, not by squashing them.

Compare these authoritarian bullies with the quote from Sun Tzu's *The Art of War*, "Regard your soldiers as your children and they will follow you into the deepest valleys; look upon them as you own beloved sons, and they will stand by you even into death."[112]

Which one is more efficient?

---

110 https://www.frontiersin.org/articles/10.3389/fnhum.2018.00199/full#:~:text=Self%2Dreferential%20processing%20refers%20to,cue%20associated%20with%20the%20self.
111 https://www.ccohs.ca/oshanswers/psychosocial/bullying.html
112 Translation from Lionel Giles, Chapter X, line 25

Respect and trust are earned. By wanting to impose respect and trust, they lose it all. Often these people have forgotten or never seen a wise quote from Niccolo Machiavelli announcing, "It is not titles that honor men but men that honor titles.[113]

---

113 Goodreads.com, Niccolo Machiavelli Quotes

CHAPTER 29

MANAGING PERCEPTION

ANYBODY REMEMBER THE MOVIE *Dead Poets Society*? Carpe Diem, seize the day.[114] All sorts of issues may come our way; challenges and setbacks appear, and, as managers, we need to deal with them. As they moralize in the movie, when you don't like what you are seeing from a certain normal, and accepted point of view like seated on school benches change your perspective and look at the issue from a different angle, like standing on the desks. Most situations can be seen from the "normal" standpoint and be interpreted as such. Others can, with a little effort and training, be seen from various angles until one finds an angle that makes the particular situation joyful, energetic, and positive. It allows one to seize the opportunity, seize the day. Carpe diem.

Chinese Story

To highlight the above introduction, let's explore this story in the *Huai-nan-tse*:[115]

114 https://www.litcharts.com/lit/dead-poets-society/themes/life-death-and-carpe-diem
115 https://www.britannica.com/topic/Huainanzi

"An old man and his son lived in an abandoned fortress of the side of the hill. Their only possession of value was a horse.

One day the horse ran away. The neighbors came to offer sympathy. "That's really bad," they said. "How do you know?" asked the old man.

The next day, the horse returned, bringing with it several wild horses. The old man and his son shut them all inside the gate. The neighbors hurried over. "That's really good," they said. "How do you know?" asked the old man.

The following day, the son tried riding one of the wild horses, fell off, and broke his leg. The neighbors came around as soon as they heard the news. "That's really bad," they said. "How do you know?" asked the old man.

The day after that, the army came through, forcing the local young men into service to fight a faraway battle against the northern barbarians. Many of them would never return. But the son couldn't go because he'd broken his leg."

And so, I ask you, what is bad? What is good?

The project you are managing has a budget cost.... Bad? Or does this give the opportunity to re-engineer it, streamline it, and simplify it?

One of your team members leaves.... Bad? Or does this give the opportunity to promote a young talent, train someone, and reorganize the group?

The promising technology does not work.... Bad? The partner did not deliver.... Bad?

All those examples, and many more, are bad from the normal, standard point of view. As an efficient manager, we learn to seek, hunt, and find how the evolution of the situation can be used to our advantage, or how a "bad" can actually be a "good." The first step is seeing things as they are, not with the impression that it is bad because that is the first, obvious, and de facto impression. Once seen as it is, without that historical, sociological, or emotional filter, we can then make the most of it.

As my favorite turtle, Master Oogway, states in *Kung Fu Panda*, "There is just news. There is no good or bad."[116]

Circumstances

Just as any situation can be interpreted and perceived from various angles until we find the angle that helps our managerial objectives and finality, it is the same with people.

To demonstrate, think of any adjective that is normally thought of as a "quality," like generosity, benevolence, and courage. You can find a few situations where those qualities become pitfalls. Take any default quality: cowardice, greed, and weakness can prove useful in a few situations and even save your life. As a manager, don't look for qualities, but learn what your team and your resources can do. How, when, and why, and make the most of them. Turn

---

116 https://www.quotes.net/mquote/118593

qualities, defaults, aptitudes, behaviors, and attitudes to your advantage to serve the finality.

Many managers try their hardest to maintain an image to show that they "know." They are in control, and they have the solutions. Truth is, maintaining an image tends to get in the way of seeing what's there, and without it, how can one make the most of it?

Now, if we learn to see what is there, if we learn to realize that "bad" is not necessarily bad, and that "good" is not necessarily good, then what about "small," "hard," "painful," "sad," "long," etc.? Aren't those all tags we give based on our impression, the learned and socially encouraged ones?

The efficient manager does not perceive. He sees, uses, and optimizes. He now succeeds with ease since he is free of maintaining image or illusionary biases.

Carpe diem.

CHAPTER 30

SMART MANAGEMENT

I'VE WRITTEN A CHAPTER previously on coaching,[117] in which I stated that depending on the situation, you can coach by being in front, side by side, or in the back of whoever you need or want to coach. Let me now expand on those notions.

Being Smart. Is That Coaching?

A lot of human resources folks and managers nowadays use yearly SMART objectives.[118] SMART is a mnemonic acronym for an objective that is:

- Specific
- Measurable
- Achievable
- Realistic
- Time-bound

These objectives are given, and throughout the year, the employee needs to try to remember them and progress.

---

117 Chapter 18
118 https://corporatefinanceinstitute.com/resources/management/smart-goal/

Often the employee completes these on their own or with a short external training, which usually has very little retention levels.

In addition, these SMART objectives usually relate to numbers since they need to be measurable and do not take into consideration the bigger picture. Here are some examples:

- To achieve a 20 percent net profit by May 31.
- To generate 30 percent revenue from online sales in the current fiscal year.
- To recruit three new people to the finance team by the beginning of the calendar year.

If a pandemic hits, or the online sales program gets cancelled, or you hire three but five resign, say goodbye to SMART objectives.

Sometimes there are midyear reviews to check the progress of the objectives. A lot of managers, not wanting to hurt the feelings or demotivate the employee, will pretend to see significant progress and will tweak the metric to make it shine, or more. This is regardless of the employee's objective achievements if otherwise they are doing a great job.

What is the employee really learning? What type of coaching does that manager really do? If a big, unexpected contract comes in and the objective is reached after a few months, then what? There are so many pitfalls of these objectives, but they make short-term life for lazy managers much easier and give key performance indicators (KPIs) to human resources, who love to implement them. Of course, these objectives refer to, well, objectives, or goals. As we have discussed in this chapter goals have much less efficient management potential and flexibility than a finality.

But what about objectives to really train, grow, and make your team progress? That brings us to Smart Coaching.

Smart Coaching Instead of Smart Objectives

Speaking of finality, this chapter discussed the importance of knowing our finality, but also the finality of our employees, colleagues, bosses, partners, and suppliers. This is to make them progress toward their finality while serving ours.

As such, the best way to truly coach is to create what I call a Finality Matrix. Let's take employee A to illustrate. Employee A is a team leader in our project, but not our direct report. His finality may be expressed as "building the best team to increase output while increasing innovation." Whether expressed or not, the efficient manager can easily guess the finality based on corporate finalities and function/group/position of the person. Knowing this and knowing our own finality will make it easy to see what this team leader does well and where he could improve, what he could realize and be aware of, his strategies and tactics, and more. All this so he can cruise toward his finality and help ours effortlessly. So, the Finality Matrix could look like this:

Table 2: Finality matrix example

Fact	Managerial actions	Managerial results*
Has difficulty talking to executives	Create reasons and excuses to have him be in safe, informal meetings, with friendly executives. Assist him in meeting preparation, etc.	Make him realize he is getting better
Delegates too much, etc.	Give him more direct ownership. Show him his importance, etc.	Track his progress to stimulate discussions around ownership

* Each "**Managerial Result**" creates a new "**Fact**," which means something has changed or is in motion. This new "**Fact**" takes a new line in the table above, with whatever is left and whatever is new.

Once we have such a matrix, either written or mentally, and we get used to it, every single direct interaction with this person has an operational meaning (complete a task, do this, tell me about that…). But it also has a managerial dimension, or put differently, a coaching dimension. For example, he has difficulties talking to executives (line 1 of the above table). In addition to the simple managerial action written in the table, you could easily:

· Invite him when you are talking to executives and ask him to evaluate you so you get feedback.

· Invite yourself to his executive meetings and give him feedback.

Just informal notifications **like** at the cafeteria, saying things like: "I had to talk to this executive and knowing he likes baseball, I used that language and talked about the game last night …" It is to allow him to take tips **and** techniques from your experience.

This is all **direct**. You can easily do **it indirectly** as well. Say you get along great with one of the executives; ask him to act, help, **or** intervene, since this will help with whatever project you are working on and he, as an executive, will benefit by thinking about his own finality.

For the efficient manager, every interaction is a pretext to manage and to progress in the direction of his finality. Coaching, from all its angles, front, side, back, direct, or indirect, helps people grow. Those very people will pull you toward your finality. But to do this, you need to know where each resource is **and** how and why you want and need them to progress. The rest is just a game.

CHAPTER 31

ROOT MANAGEMENT

THE CONCEPT OF ROOT-CAUSE ANALYSIS[119] is a well-known one and is typically applied in most engineering firms and in R&D organizations.

The question is if it is so popular and efficient in design, engineering, **and** science, why is it typically completely ignored from a management perspective?

Scratching the Surface

Root-cause analysis is thorough and deep to make sure that whatever solution is developed addresses the issue. Several tools exist to do this analysis. Some of the most used are the fishbone diagram (Ishikawa diagrams[120]) and the failure mode and effects analysis (FMEA[121]). Another approach is "the five whys."[122] These tools and techniques allow us to go deep into the problem, to the root itself, and address the fundamental cause of the issue, not only address the consequence.

---

119 https://www.tableau.com/learn/articles/root-cause-analysis
120 https://www.mindmanager.com/en/features/ishikawa-diagram
121 https://asq.org/quality-resources/fmea
122 https://www.mindtools.com/a3mi00v/5-whys

However, in the management world, such tools are not used. Here are two examples that were submitted to me recently to show the typical managerial approach:

1. Turnaround is quite high, and executives and HR are worried. They launch a companywide survey about happiness, engagement, trust, and so on. Regardless, if there are 20 or 100 questions, these remain generic questions, and the answers are averaged per department per branch. An average of generalities is often scored from 1 to 10. Afterward, these same executives and HR people use these averaged generalities, interpret them from their point of view (discussed in part in this chapter), and offer even more general "solutions" that ultimately decrease the mobilization. Since they do not address specifics, they reduce the employees' trust in management. Good conscience, absent or negative impact.

2. People complain that there are too many meetings and that they do not have the time to do "real work." Root causes can include:
   o Cultural behaviors in the company
   o Difficulty making decisions due to always needing a consensus
   o Always needing to escalate and having to prepare for escalation
   o Roles and responsibilities are poorly defined

So, the company issues a policy of "No Friday morning meetings allowed" only to address the consequences and not the root cause. The result is that all the Friday a.m. meetings are shifted else-where in the agendas, which are already full since this was the initial issue. This leads to meetings during lunch hours, after normal working hours, and so on. Of course, this adds major complexity to meetings that include people from various time zones.

In both cases, there is no depth of understanding. The direct managers did not understand the various, individual fundamental issues, and a generic patch was proposed. If you call your doctor with a pain in the left arm and he tells you, without any tests and without analysis, "Go home and put ice on it for 12 minutes every hour," that won't repair the bone or prevent a cardiac issue.

From Consciousness to Action

As I discussed in one of my first chapters there are no reci-pes for management. Global generic solutions do not solve individual, specific worries and issues. Yet time and again, managers use time and resources to set generalities that fail to achieve results, and they say to their bosses and con-science, "Look, I tried; I did my best." Efforts wasted, time wasted, results underwhelming. These are not the ways of the Efficient Manager.

I discussed in several chapters so far that the more you know a situation, the better you can foresee it, prevent it, dissect it, and exploit it. The key word is KNOW.

Yet, this requires time, effort, and analysis. Often managers use this pattern unconsciously because of a lack of time or ego. When I am made aware of something, I take action/make a decision.

There is a direct link from being aware of something to taking action.

- Sales are down; Let's do a promotional campaign.
- People are leaving; Let's make a survey.
- Baby is crying; Let's give him a pacifier.
- Plants are dying; Give them more water.

In other words: A problem is being manifested; a solution is proposed. Where is the "understanding" part?

The awareness-action path is a shortcut that makes people pretend they are effective, managerial, and smart. But it is a shortcut that is very costly and in total opposition with efficiency. The true path of the efficient manager should be awareness–comprehension–action. The comprehension part is the human root cause analysis, or the why of the why of the why. This concept is universal and prescriptive. It can be summarized by the following: once we are aware that a situation, an opportunity, a reality exists, the more we understand it and the more the following action will be accurate, efficient, and relevant. The action will embrace the flow and allow transformation. Our main objective should be to achieve a complete objective understanding of the situation to lead us to many more accomplishments than all the random actions.

To quote two parts on Sun Tzu's *The Art of War*:

- "If we know that our own men are in a condition to attack but are unaware that the enemy is not open to attack, we have gone only halfway towards victory. If we know that the enemy is open to attack but are unaware that our own men are not in a condition to attack, we have gone only halfway towards victory. If we know that the enemy is open to attack, and also know that our men are in a condition to attack but are unaware that the nature of the ground makes fighting impracticable, we have still gone only halfway towards victory. Hence the experienced soldier, once in motion, is never bewildered; once he has broken camp, he is never at a loss."[123]
- "What enables the wise sovereign and the good general to strike and conquer, and achieve things beyond the reach of ordinary men, is foreknowledge.[124]

The solution, or the path, is within the situation, and the only way to see it through is by deep understanding.

---

123 Translation from Lionel Giles, Chapter X, lines 27-30
124 Translation from Lionel Giles, Chapter XIII, line 4

CHAPTER 32

MANAGING HEROES

THERE ARE MANY FORMS of heroism. Doctors and police officers are daily heroes because they protect and save all of us regularly. In a more generic term, a hero is someone who saves the day. *Collins Dictionary* defines a hero as "someone who has done something brave, new, or good, and who is therefore greatly admired by a lot of people."[125] One could see a hero as the one who saves the day, in the words of Mighty Mouse.[126]

If a hero is someone who saves the day, what about the hero in the manager's team? What about the manager-hero?

Workplace Heroes

Let's get to this last idea of heroism, someone who saves the day, or saves the situation, the sale, the project, the key employee, or the company itself. Oh yes, this person has all the praise, the glory, and the recognition, so this is necessarily seen positively by colleagues and superiors. So, all good, right?

---

125 https://www.collinsdictionary.com/dictionary/english/hero
126 https://mightymouse.fandom.com/wiki/Mighty_Mouse

But the most important question is not "Who saved the day?" but the most important question is "Why did the day need saving?" as referenced in my previous chapter on Root Cause Management.[127]

Most of us, at least in occidental countries, have grown up in a world where praised and prideful heroes are held in high regard, either by cartoons and comic books, or championship game MVPs. Lost in the praise and the pride of having the day saved, we focus much more on heroic action than on the reason why heroism was required to start with.

We cherish and love our heroes; we want them on our teams, and we want to be the next hero. We long for that praise and recognition.

But the true question, in my humble opinion, is if a workplace situation needed heroism to be saved, how good were the plan and strategy beforehand? And who was responsible for that plan and strategy? A good strategy must not involve heroism, so aren't most of these cases of heroism a clear sign of managerial deficiency?

Going back to the Collins Dictionary definition, heroes combat adversity through feats of bravery. Where is the efficiency in there? How good is a hero manager, really, since he let the situation degrade until a hero was required?

---

127 Chapter 31

Managerial Implications

Efficient managers do not seek out glory or play the hero's role. Sun Tzu states in *The Art of War*, "Neither is it the acme of excellence if you fight and conquer and the whole Empire says, Well done!"[128] This is because if someone realizes you've done well, then the victory was not built in the natural flow and evolution. It needed a hero.

That being said, not everyone on your team, in your network of allies and spies, is an efficient manager. Most of them will want praise and recognition, to have a chance to shine. This is certainly a trait the efficient manager can use. Remember, when we talk about management, we talk about strategically activating resources to achieve our finality with effectiveness and efficiency. In a previous chapter on ego,[129] I discussed the notion of being self-referential. To know that they want to be heard, to be a hero, to be recognized, or to do things their way, it is much easier to lean on the potential of a situation. The more we understand what makes them do certain things, the more we can make them do what needs to be done to transform the situation.

But be very careful of public praise.

Public praise means that in front of an entire group, someone is praised and recognized as the hero in the situation. While for that person it is a great feeling, contrarily,

---

128 Translation from Lionel Giles, Chapter IV, line 9
129 Chapter 28

the others may feel that they contributed as well, and are not receiving any of the glory or recognition. Some people work in the background and never play the hero's role. This can create a feeling of injustice, disappointment, and even frustration. Praise should be given individually and should be given frequently to all members of the team, to all resources and allies. As Lao Tzu puts it in the Tao-Te Ching, "By not elevating the worthy, you bring it about that people will not compete."[130]

As managers who understand this, when someone tries to tell us, "Well done," our reflex should always be to say something along the lines of, "I didn't do much, the team did it all." The *Art of War* manager is obsessed with improving their position and achieving their finality, not by themself. They want results and achievements, and they have no need for a high performer status.

Action vs. Transformation

Heroism is often based on a single set of defined, visible, and noticeable actions. The *Art of War* talks about transformation. Instead of destroying opposing forces, it is better to make them join our side. This spares our own troops and makes our army larger. Efficiency is therefore maximized.

Transformation takes time to operate. It is not seen, it is implied in a reality nobody challenges, it is part of

130 Tao Te Ching, Chapter 3, translation by Stephen Mitchell

the natural flow of things, so it is unstoppable, just like aging, nails growing, etc. But it also remains unpraised. As such, this kind of manager obtains the result without ever attracting attention, and it is totally unremarkable from the outside. They do not need to act to make things happen. Changes occur by themselves, from themselves, as consequences, or as a continuity of the process, without putting pressure on the situation or expending energy. To make things happen, they do not look to impose the effect as we do when we act, but they let the effect impose itself.

The transformation is not perceptible as it happens but is made obvious by the effects and impacts. The situation evolves so naturally, in the desired direction, by planting seeds way ahead of the process. The outcome becomes natural, and victory is easy, and no praise for the manager. And that, is the greatest praise of all.

CHAPTER 33

MANAGING DETAILS

I HAVE MENTIONED IN a previous chapter[131] a well-known proverb: "The devil is in the details." In that chapter, I discussed the importance of a coach to help every resource understand, see, learn, and optimize the details that form their job. In another chapter about terminology,[132] I detailed the differences between four typical organizational layers, from executives to directors down to managers, and finally the executors.

The importance of the proverb "the devil is in the details" in the context of visibility from one's function, is a critical aspect in efficient management.

Setting the Stage for Chaos

In the text about organizational layers, I mentioned, "A big problem, of course, is that a lot of directors used to be managers and enjoy being in the operational ... then these directors are promoted to VPs ... and chaos is taking a grip on the organization."

---

131 Chapter 18
132 Chapter 25

Isn't chaos the work of devils? Why does chaos loom in such conditions?

Let's create an analogy to explain the concept and then explore the managerial implications. A typical country, state, or city will have its executives in the form of a president, a prime minister, a governor, and a mayor. Most citizens are executors, from the baker to the banker, from the manager to the bus driver. The top layer of the organization needs to have a view of the big storylines and the major issues. They need to have an overview of what is going on in their jurisdiction. They do not know the details of the pharmacist on Second Avenue or the math teacher in any given high school. They have their level of detail, a very macro set of details. On the other hand, the math teacher knows the details of their program, their class, family, agenda, etc. But they are not fully aware of the aqueduct, trash retrieval, taxes, and police conventions that are part of the larger organization around them.

When the math teacher starts to believe they understand all of these things, they do not have a good enough view of the entire picture. So, they do not always make sense of the municipal decisions and complaints. Just like if the mayor tries to understand the details and life of every single citizen, they will never have time to manage.

In the corporate world, going to management, especially efficient management, the same concept applies.

A firm has executors like production people and electronic engineers. They know their jobs normally in heavy detail and they know why each step is taken and why this certain component is used. They are in the micro-level detail of a very narrow point of view. The executives know that production exists, and that engineering exists, but their views of the company are much broader. They know things, from finance to human resources, marketing, and way beyond the walls of the company, like customers, investors, competitors, and investment opportunities. They have a wide lens, with little depth in most, if not all, the aspects that are not directly under their responsibility.

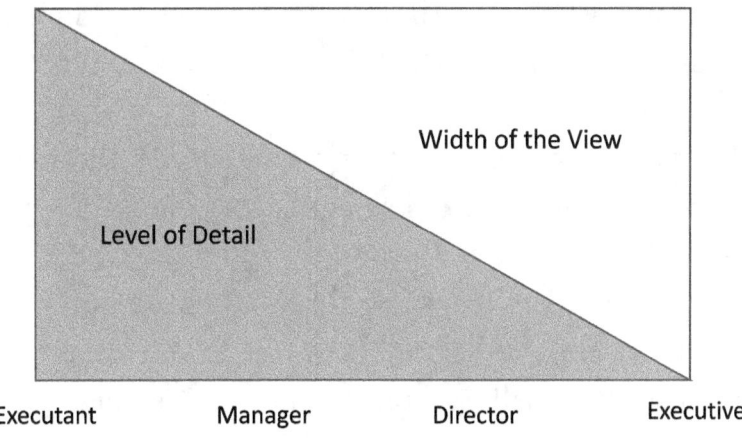

Figure 3: Level of detail vs. level of management

Just like a camera, a large field of view has few details, while a narrow field of view shows more than a single aspect.

Chaos Unleashed

Now, as I mentioned in the introduction, executors, with a high level of narrow detail knowledge, are promoted to group managers. They need to learn to have a wider view, but to let go of some level of detail, of some of what has made them great. If they learn to let go on their own, then it's awesome. But if not, their various other tasks will require them to have less time to be aware of all the details, and yet they still believe and want to be in that comfort zone. Then they challenge, play big brother,[133] second-guess, and create stagnation and sluggishness in the process. Next, they eventually become directors with an even wider view, and since they cringe on details, they will often bypass their new manager to go back to the level of detail of executors ... and so on.

Or there can be executors from outside the field of expertise, which is normal since, as they climb the ladder, the view becomes larger and more and more of that view is not from our detailed original field. If the executor is not from that field of expertise but wants to show their value or impose their will or pretend they are managing, they will go into the micro details of all the various fields under their umbrella, which puts a lot of sand in the gears and creates a lot of inefficiencies.

---

133 https://www.collinsdictionary.com/us/dictionary/english/big-brother#:~:text=People%20sometimes%20use%20Big%20Brother,%5Bdisapproval%5D

Great examples are VPs saying, "I know what my people are doing. I used to do that, and you are not doing it right," or CEOs saying, "I want to review in depth the manufacturing process of that product since I was made aware of a lot of customer complaints."

As Sun Tzu mentions in *The Art of War*, the general is on the battlefield, he knows the details of that battle, while the sovereign is not. Hence the sentence, "There are commands of the sovereign which must not be obeyed."[134] And an even more powerful one is "He will win who has the military capacity and is not interfered with by the sovereign."[135]

The competent general will win if he has no intervention from the sovereign. Let's ponder that. To reformulate, the general could win yet sovereign interference may make him lose. The competent programmers know what to do, and the competent designers and production engineers know what to do. When the boss, or the boss's boss, or anybody higher up the stack pretends they know more of the details than the one doing it, takes the right to dictate, they eventually complain and argue. That superior is not at their level of detail. They may be that sovereign interfering with victory.

The efficient manager strategically activates their resources. They do not tell them what to do.

---

134 Translation from Lionel Giles, Chapter VIII, line 3
135 Translation from Lionel Giles, Chapter III, line 17

CHAPTER 34

MANAGING THE SANDBOX PUZZLE

THE DEVIL IS IN the details. I mentioned that in the previous chapter. I also mentioned the importance of terminology[136] of roles vs. functions. I covered goals vs. finalities[137], and the importance of added value.

Taking all those ideas and concepts into consideration, let's discuss the idea of organizational restructuring when the business fails to achieve the desired level of traction, success, or profitability.

The R&R Puzzle

The corporation, with its executives, defines a structural organization, departments, and work orchestration. From there, directors and group managers define roles and responsibilities (R&R). Each job is defined more or less as a sandbox, i.e., this is what the job should do and be responsible for. It's the purpose and the "how to do it," mixing role and function in the process. For instance, during either

136 Chapter 25
137 Chapter 22

official or nonofficial discussions, a manager might mention to an underling, "As your boss, this is what I expect from you; this is your job, your function/role.

Figure 4: R&R sandbox

The ideal perception when these R&R structures are defined is that each of these sandboxes complete each other perfectly, so they have an optimum, efficient, and perfectly oiled organization. This allows the company to reach its set goals and objectives.

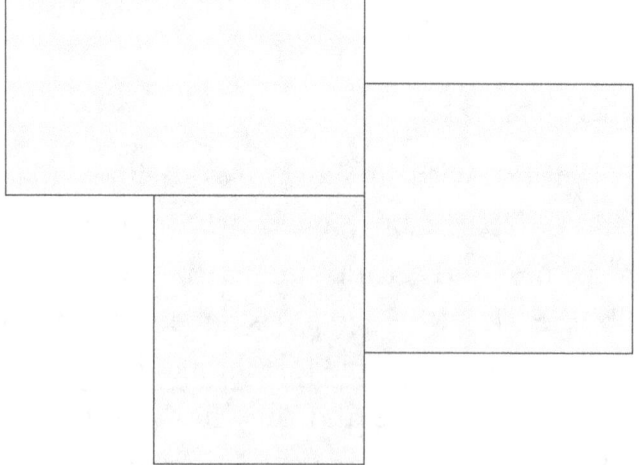

Figure 5: Perfect sandbox juxtaposition

Sandboxes Through Time

Of course, with time, the perfect model described above differs from reality: Because roles and responsibilities change and because of the different understanding of the boundaries of each sandbox, no two product owners will define a job exactly the same and do the same thing. Also, reality evolves and what was good on day 1 might not be relevant on day 2, and there are a multitude of other reasons such as role change, personal change, and the appearance of new tasks. Boxes sometimes overlap or have gaps between them. In other words, even from the day of implementation of an R&R model, there are flaws.

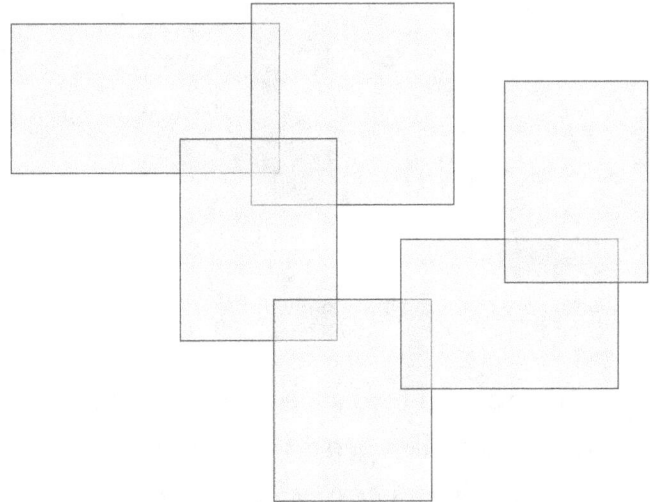

Figure 6: Sandbox juxtaposition starting to fail

Each area of overlap is either a lack of efficiency, which leads to a lack of profitability (two people doing the same thing, tasks split into different functions, etc.), or a risk that the task never gets done because each sandbox owner will believe the other one take care of it. Each gap means something that is not completed. Small overlaps and gaps may be manageable and not impact dramatically, but as time goes by, reality continues to evolve, and the pattern often intensifies.

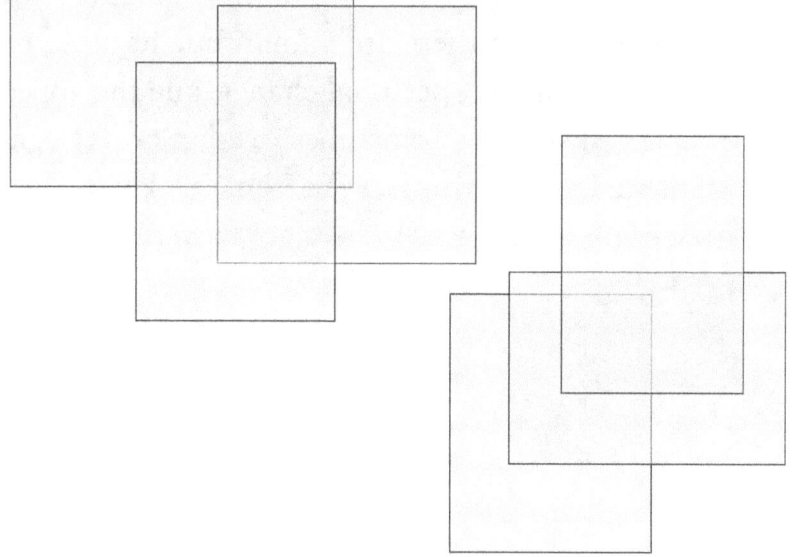

Figure 7: Sandbox overlapping and gapping.

Margins decrease because of lack of efficiency, projects are longer, confusion gets installed with questions like "Who does what? Is that my job?" Customers are served poorly because of all the gaps, and so on. Heroism needs to occur to fill the gaps, and we know what an efficient manager thinks about heroism.

- Some companies give spot bonuses for heroics, extraordinary performances, thus recognizing and encouraging gaps.
- Others may create functions to fill the gaps, eventually creating extra overlaps and extra decreases of profitability.
- Higher management can be tempted to say, "Strategically our vision is great but we (meaning the employee), did not execute it properly," which means non-executives did not do their job.

These gaps and overlaps may lead to burnouts and departures, and/or new reorganizations, meaning new sandboxes and a new puzzle created, thus restarting the cycle, and not addressing the fundamental issues as discussed in Chapter 31. While the new puzzle is being figured out by middle-level managers and employees, new gaps appear. Sometimes, I would say quite often, the gaps are engineered in the new puzzle since the ones creating the puzzle do not have the global picture and oversee details, and the devil is in those details. As these new gaps and overlaps appear, the pattern restarts, leading to new reorganizations, and eventually maybe even the downfall of the company, unless several heroes emerge.

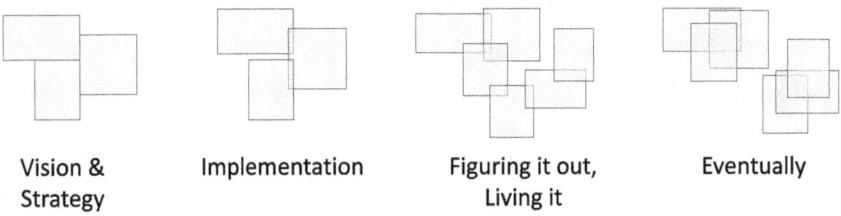

| Vision & Strategy | Implementation | Figuring it out, Living it | Eventually |

Figure 8: Sandboxes vs. reality evolution.

Boundaries

This is true for entire organizations, but also for smaller teams. The more a team member has closed boundaries, the more this creates silos, removes the person from the global finality, and favors a deluge of excuses and gaps. The solution is, of course, to lose sandboxes and fix roles and responsibilities. It is instead good to have a finality, enforce added value work if and only if this serves the finality. It also needs control mechanisms. As Sun Tzu points out, "Fighting with a large army under your command is nowise different from fighting with a small one: it is merely a question of instituting signs and signals."[138]

---

138 Translation from Lionel Giles, Chapter V, line 2

CHAPTER 35

MANAGING SILOS

IN EVERY COMPANY I have worked with and more that I know of, the most important issue that needs to be addressed or that limits growth and innovation, are silos. Working in silos, or every department for itself, or to the extreme, every person for themselves, people are submerged with tasks and highly overworked. The simple action of documenting and sharing is seen as a luxurious overhead, and luxury is often the first thing to be dropped.

To quote John Darnielle: *"Silos are the great hidden constant of the industrialized world."*[139]

How can the efficient manager work with these silos to optimize his throughput?

The Story of the Baker

A friend of mine once told me that after a certain amount of time, work, job, or activity brings on a certain state of mind. I, for example, have never been a baker by trade. I do not *think* like a baker. Yet if I were to start a job as a baker, at first, I would learn the tricks of the trade. After

---

139 Goodreads.com, John Darnielle Quotes

a while, I would start to embody the baker. I would think like a baker. I would see flavors, flour, butter, and all delicacies from a different viewpoint, associate smells, and tastes, and so on. Not all bakers think alike, of course, but they all think as bakers. Same for police officers, hockey players, etc.

This seems to be true for most jobs. In a high-tech enterprise, for example, a CFO thinks like a CFO, a marketing specialist thinks about marketing, a production manager thinks about how to produce better, an engineer thinks about how to design and innovate, and a salesperson thinks about how to increase sales.

So, if this is true for individuals and "titles" and "functions," I make the case that the same is true for attitudes and behaviours. Regardless of his role, a new employee who starts in an environment where there are silos will start to think in silos, from their job's perspective at least. As such, just stating that we need and should end silos is not enough.

A Case for Altruism

In a previous chapter[140] I mentioned the importance of altruism for personal happiness. Altruism has a documented and proven benefit on individuals at that level, as I demonstrated in that chapter. Altruism and cooperation are the opposite of silos. Trying to tell employees of the

---

140 Chapter 16

importance of sharing and working as a team will not change the habits and culture. Breaking down someone else's house will not make them become better members of the community. Telling me how to be a baker will not make me one. I need to live it, experience it, and become it.

As such, the best way to make people learn to work together is to make them work together. This will eventually lead to a shared state of mind of cooperation.

The efficient manager can and should not only promote, but create situations, or excuses, for people to work together. Instead of, for example, seeing a project as part marketing, part cost, part electronics, part software, part everything, he must see the project as an entity and make sure each part of that entity is aware of the others and offer each other help, i.e., How can my part help your part be better so the entity is better?

Altruistic Brothers

Imagine these two project update meeting scenarios:

1. The project manager goes over each function for an executive report on the function and asks relevant questions to clarify any issues.
2. The project manager goes over each function for an executive report on the function. They then ask other functions how that helps them, if they need anything different, or if they can help and support that function.

Like brothers in arms. Like my favorite Disney character, Stitch,[141] says often, "Ohana means family: Nobody gets left behind or forgotten."[142]

After a few of such meetings as the one described in the second scenario, naturally when any function speaks, others chip in and want to help. You don't break the silos; you give your employees a reason to come out of theirs.

You could even push it one step further:

3. The project manager goes around asking each function for an executive report on another function and what they will do to help that other function.

This forces everyone to know what everyone else is doing, and how they can help them succeed. They share their progress and their ideas, and eventually this goes above and beyond the team meeting. Everyone starts to care about the success of the others on the team, camaraderie increases, and silos become irrelevant; they disappear. A sense of brotherhood is born.

Speaking of brotherhood, the US Navy SEALs[143] are one of the elite forces in the world. A team attitude and integrity are valued qualities of SEALs. No matter how strong and determined a SEAL, few missions are successful without teamwork. Much of the training emphasizes the development

141 https://disney.fandom.com/wiki/Stitch
142 Goodreads.com, Lilo and Stitch Quotes
143 https://www.navy.com/seals

of brotherhood and camaraderie. Focusing on the needs of others and supporting fellow SEALs help members fight through the pain and mental burdens of training and intense missions. Altruism is built into their world, the mentality and state of mind of the best of the best.

Trying to break silos is like taking a hammer and trying to break down houses so that everyone starts to talk to each other and become great friends. But by doing this, each household will turn back on itself for security and start building up greater walls again. Through altruism you gradually invite people to visit other households, to get to know them, spend time with them, and start to care for them. Now, you do not even need to break down the walls. The walls become naturally useless through the natural evolution of the situation. Silos fade away.

Altruism is the key to self-happiness, but also to removing silos. But it needs a push, a seed from the efficient manager to get the wheel turning. Since after a certain time, a certain job brings a certain behavior; the "altruism" job becomes behaviour.

To quote the Dalai Lama, the essence of altruism is well captured. He states, "Interdependence is a fundamental law of nature. Even tiny insects survive by cooperating with each other. We need to cultivate a genuine sense of responsibility and a sincere concern for the welfare of others."[144]

---

144 https://bestdalailamaquotes.tumblr.com/post/114896971437/interdependence-is-a-fundamental-law-of-nature

Breaking silos doesn't come by forcing the break or trying to explain why for the corporation it is important. It comes naturally by replacing the silos with altruism.

CHAPTER 36

MANAGING DIFFICULTIES

WHY ARE THINGS DIFFICULT? Because of a lack of knowledge or maybe a lack of preparation? As I concluded in a recent chapter,[145] easy and difficult are perspectives, depending on skills, experience, mindset, and preparation. While skills are learned, experience comes with time, so mindset and preparation are tools a manager, especially the efficient manager, has at their disposal. How to go above and beyond is difficult. To make things easy, or at least appear easy, I refer to Sun Tzu's *The Art of War*: "A clever fighter is one who not only wins but excels in winning with ease.[146]"

Perspectives

There are two main ways to approach this notion of difficulty:

- We can be confident people, knowing we have resources, skills, experiences, and to have everything quite simple. Therefore, we assume things will be easy.

---

145 Chapter 29
146 Translation from Lionel Giles, Chapter IV, line 11

- We can always assume things will be difficult and prepare as such.

Now, the person who believes, either by ego, experience, or other reasons, that things will be easy, when they do, in fact, turn out to be easy, they are content. However, life is often more complicated than what we hope for. Things get complicated and are not as easy as thought of initially. As such, many tasks thought to be easy end up being "less easy" and somewhat difficult. We operate in a constant difficult space.

For the person who assumes things will be difficult, a worse scenario is that they are indeed difficult. Since they were anticipating them as such, they are prepared, and because of this preparation, they end up being easy.

As Lao Tzu mentions in the *Tao Te Chung*, "Those who regard many things as easy will necessarily end up with many difficulties. Therefore, even the Sage regards things as difficult, and as a result, in the end he has no difficulty."[147]

Taking the position described above, to assume things will be difficult, and therefore, always succeed with ease, more ease than anticipated, leads to two things:

- Self-confidence because things were easy.
- Confidence from teams, colleagues, supervisors, and stakeholders, as you always have the answers, are in control, are

---

147 Tao Te Ching, Chapter 63, translation by Stephen Mitchell

never caught off-guard and never appear shaky. You become a trusted advisor, and the more you are trusted, the easier the path forward after.

As such, if you are always ready for everything, you never need to prepare yourself.

When you are fluid, when you read the situations and know everybody's finalities, concerns, and positions, it is easy to prepare for their actions and reactions. To see events unfold before they are occurring, and to prepare for that unfolding by having the answers, the solutions or the means to steer the conversation to a more friendly ground will have the same effect. Yet this will never be sufficient, as people, by nature, have an unpredictable side to them, as described in Chapter 5. Expect the unexpected, and when you are ready for it, it is not unexpected anymore.

Being prepared means you have many options that you can turn to if or when you need them. Better to have too many options than too few. Options are choices, choices are power and leverage.

Having that state of mind, or assuming difficulty, puts us in a state where we take nothing for granted, and we give our full attention to details, words, and behaviors. We "work hard" in order to not work hard when difficulties arise. We address difficulties when they are simple. Whereas someone who takes for granted that things will be easy may be underprepared. They are sloppy, lazy, and get themselves into a lot of trouble, shaking the confidence of those around them. We all had that presentation where we thought it would be a walk in the park only to have that killer question come out and throw the whole presentation into Neverland.

What about Stress?

I often hear the argument that if you always take for granted and expect that things will be difficult, doesn't it create a lot of unnecessary stress, always being confronted with difficult tasks? To that I answer, what is the most stressful, preparing in case things get complicated, or dealing with complicated things totally unprepared?

Assuming something will be difficult is not creating stress, it is addressing a situation before it becomes stressful or before it has the opportunity to take uncontrollable proportions. You always ask yourself questions, create scenarios and "What ifs" based on your acquired knowledge and your attention to reality. That way, stress is completely avoided. As mentioned above, the more you do this, the more you build confidence around you, and the more those people around you will believe, have faith, and have trust, the less they will challenge and be more receptive to ideas and suggestions. Preparation is not a stressful moment; it allows us to remove stress during execution.

Always tell yourself, "It will be difficult." Always prepare accordingly, and as the clever fighter you will excel at winning with ease. To quote the Dalai Lama, "All suffering is caused by ignorance."[148] Assume things will be hard, prepare in consequence, and stay informed.

---

148 Goodreads.com, Dalai Lama XIV Quotes

CHAPTER 37

MANAGING HABITS

OUR CHARACTER AND BEHAVIOR today are essentially the sum of our habits. These shape our life path. As the Shaolin mantra goes, thoughts lead to words. This leads to actions, then habits, and finally character, for these to define your life. So, habits are central to who we are.

Habits are done on autopilot; they require very little brain power and processing effort. They are, therefore, the pinnacle of efficiency, something the efficient manager should love.

However, I often get this comment after group interventions: "hmmm, what you say is interesting and it will get me to think and ponder." Yet seldom do behaviors change. New Year's resolutions are a perfect example of this phenomenon; it clearly makes sense, but there is no follow-through.

Why is that, and how can we manage habits to become more efficient?

The Habit Loop

A little bit of the loop was discussed in the Root Management Chapter.[149] It is important to understand how habits are formed and why we resist their change. The more we understand, the more we can act with purpose and success.

Habits are created from repetition and consistency. The more we do, the more it becomes natural. Often people try to add or change the habit by changing, creating, or removing a "do": Do this more, do that less, do this instead of that. Unfortunately, this system often fails.

Every habit starts with a psychological pattern called the "habit loop."[150] This loop is made of three steps:

- The cue or the trigger is something that tells your brain to go into pilot mode and let the behavior be.
- The routine, which is the behavior itself, or the "do."
- The reward, something that your brain likes and helps to remember the habit loop in the future. A level of dopamine is released, thus creating a pleasant feeling, the reward.

Once the behavior becomes a habit, the brain can completely shut down the decision-making part for that particular action/behavior. It becomes an unconscious and energy-efficient action. We become unaware of the trigger

---

149 Chapter 31
150 https://habitica.fandom.com/wiki/The_Habit_Loop#:~:text=Edit-,The%20Habit%20
Loop,.%22%20%2D%20Duhigg%2C%20C.

itself and have no need for the reward either. We just do it. But until this is solidified, the habit loop is crucial.

Like most things discussed so far, misunderstanding the loop will lead to trying the second step above, leading to failure more often than not. It just happens that step two is the most demanding of the steps.

The simplest ways to implement this are:

- **Identify a cue**: When this will happen, like "when I meet this person", "when I see this," "when I am at …," then the routine kicks in.
- **Identify the reward for the behavior**: Why do I want to implement this new habit and what am I trying to answer or satisfy?

Then we start adding the behavior.

Helping the Loop

As previously mentioned, a habit comes from repetition and consistency. To implement a new habit based on the steps above, the cue or trigger needs to happen regularly and with consistency. Something that happens monthly will be much harder to create as a habit than something that happens three times a day. For example, each time I sit down to eat, I will …

The reward needs to be a real one that truly generates satisfaction. Trying to build a new habit because it looks interesting, or because our boss asks us, has very little reward. As such, an important part of the habit loop is the reason, or the "why" that you want to add a new habit. The manager wishing to be more efficient is an okay reason. The manager who wants to save 30 percent of his workweek is much more concrete. The manager who wants to save 30 percent of his workweek to start learning something else that will get him a promotion in six months is much more rewarding. Fundamentally, the stronger the "why," the more each little habit victory brings us closer to that. Each time the trigger comes, the reward is potentially powerful. The brain likes rewards and dopamine and will therefore do the task. Dopamine is addictive; When the cue comes, we want the reward, so we solidify the habit.

Expanding the Loop

Now that we understand how habits are created and solidified, we, if we want to change our habits, remove those we do not like, or modify/replace them to become better managers.

Not only this, but managers have resources at their disposal, namely direct reports, like allies, spies, partners, and more. Do we love everything about these reports? Do we wish Paul would be a bit more like this and Mary a bit more like that?

When we are their direct managers, I often see these questions built into yearly objectives, as described in Chapter 32. When they are not direct reports, the subordinates just discuss and complain about them to their boss, or they just learn to live with them as they are.

Understanding habits opens up a constellation of possibilities. You no longer have the need to try to change habits; instead, you need to create triggers and rewards. The habits will, with time, shift by themselves.

This is critically important for managers, so let me repeat it: Create triggers and rewards, and the habits will change by themselves.

If Mary doesn't speak enough during meetings? Set a speaking order so she is always after Paul and give credit to her interventions. Before you know it, she will contribute on her own.

Loops are repeatable, predictable, and energy efficient. Use them for your own development and to develop others around you.

CHAPTER 38

MANAGING CHAOS

HAVE YOU EVER EXPERIENCED chaos in the work-place, either because of sudden growth, restructuring, change of mandate, key people leaving, unclear definitions, and more? Everything seems more complicated and longer to achieve. Everyone wants to be a manager or person in power, and they issue orders left and right. The more that is said, the less that actually gets done.

Welcome to chaos. But as an efficient manager, shouldn't we say, "Welcome chaos"?

The Chaos and Order Dance

It is funny that when everything is in perfect order, less order comes. In other words, there is some level of chaos. Yet in total chaos, only less chaos or some level of order can be made. They follow each other forever. The efficient manager knows this, and knows that when there is too much order, sooner or later chaos will be born. So, they prepare themselves for that outcome. When in chaos, eventual order will come, so the efficient manager prepares with this knowledge in mind.

Strangely enough, one continuously has to thank the presence of chaos because that is where all the potential lies. The full glass has no more potential, but the empty glass has infinite potential available. Every restriction can only lead to privilege. Having all the privileges can only lead to restrictions. Knowing that chaos has much more potential than order, we say, "Thank you, chaos, you always give the efficient manager the edge."

In chaos, nothing is in order, everything is in constant motion and movement. Herein lies the potential.

As Sun Tzu says perfectly, "*In the midst of chaos, there is also opportunity.*"[151]

So how do we tap into that potential?

Chaos, the Infinite Well of Potential

As mentioned before, when chaos is present, only order can come. In this sense, anything you do that brings a perceived sense of order, will be seen positively and be embraced. This is a perfect time to shape relations, procedures, and behaviors to best serve your finality. Something will happen, will be decided, or will change from higher management in the attempt to get back to a better order. It is much easier to seed a new course of action upstream than try to force the change of direction of something already at top speed. Favorable changes will occur by themselves and from themselves as a consequence and a continuity of returning to order.

---

151 Goodreads.com, Sun Tzu Quotes

When chaos is present, more chaos is hardly possible. If so, it is hardly seen, and in times like these, it is the perfect moment to try new things, experiment, trial and error. It is the perfect moment to learn about how things, reality, people, and events react. Chaotic times are perfect to learn and test oneself or others.

The efficient manager is always looking for circumstances to improve their situation. This may be thought of as a favorable moment that reality unexpectedly provides. But luck and faith have nothing to do with the circumstances and the occasion. They are simply the most adequate moments to intervene in the ongoing process, the moment where the most minimal effort will start the greatest favorable transformation. In the context of a transformation, an occasion is nothing more than a step in a process that time has prepared, and that the manager has recognized and seen. Chaos is an unparalleled favorable circumstance.

More importantly, what can be seen as chaos by many, may have patterns or hidden patterns. Nevertheless, they are still patterns. They are unseen by those who just struggle to survive in the chaos, unseen by those whose responsibility is to bring order back. "The forest is unseen when too close to the tree," as the expression goes. The efficient manager can easily, either directly or with their network, ask questions, poke around, and see and identify the patterns.

Once the patterns are seen, they are like rivers, following a predictable path. The floating leaf will be carried by this river effortlessly, and just like the efficient manager, it can be carried by the current of the patterns. It is their natural evolution that the others don't see, too busy damning chaos, while the manager is using it as leverage.

Therefore, one of the best things to do during these times of chaos is observe, learn, and identify in order to foresee and predict. Observation is not about thinking or comparing, it is about how things are, how they are moving and evolving. Observing brings clarity. Use your network of spies and allies to question and learn about the chaos from their perspectives, to picture the full extent. Curiosity leads to answers, so always be in the state of asking and never stop questioning. Particularly, don't give too much of your knowledge and conclusions, as the whole purpose of these tips is to have the edge in the situation.

The answer is often in the situation itself, provided that one understands the situation completely from their perspective and from as many perspectives as possible. Links and patterns emerge, and from chaos comes newfound order and simplicity. Always try to simplify.

I love the acronym KISS, "Keep It Simple, Stupid." This is a design principle noted by the US Navy in 1960, and it is a principle that most systems work best with if they are kept simple. As such, "in simplicity lies most of the answers."[152] When times of chaos are upon us, many look to both sides to see everything going wrong and try to solve everything at once. They get overwhelmed by the growing complexity of the situation.

Ask questions; dig and be curious; simplify, find patterns, and surf on those patterns. Like Confucius said, "He who asks a question is a fool for a minute. He who does not ask a question is a fool for life."[153] This is how to progress effortlessly in a field of headless chickens. At the end, through this transformation and evolution, what could have been accidental becomes unavoidable, and without needing to rely on a risky action, effort is minimal.

---

152 https://www.interaction-design.org/literature/article/kiss-keep-it-simple-stupid-a-design-principle
153 Goodreads.com, Confucius Quotes

CHAPTER 39

MANAGING INFLUENCES

SOMETIMES AS MANAGERS, TO move toward your finality you need things to happen that can only be triggered by the influence and the decision of someone else. Yet it is not natural for that person to trigger it. As mentioned in Managing the Ultimate Efficiency,[154] you can build in this decision in the natural flow of things simply by understanding the situation. However, this can take some time; the acorn will eventually become an oak, but can you afford to wait? This is where efficient managerial influence comes into play.

Direct vs. Indirect

We mentioned in several previous chapters differences between direct and indirect. Sun Tzu in *The Art of War* discusses this in length, starting with, "In all fighting, the direct method may be used for joining battle, but indirect methods will be needed in order to secure victory."[155]

---

154 Chapter 17
155 Translation from Lionel Giles, Chapter V, line 5

Direct Influence

This method, as the name implies, is when the manager (M) tries to influence the target (T) directly.

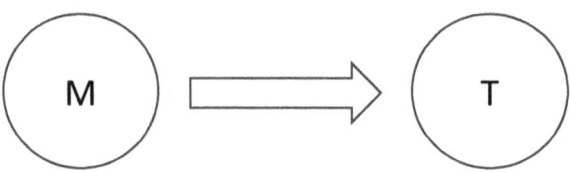

Figure 9: Direct influence

Conditions for success:

- You are an ally to the target (allies are defined in Chapter 14).
- The target is an ally to you.
- You and your direct influence have a compelling argument that benefits the target for doing whatever you are asking, hoping, or insinuating.

The risk, with any direct action, is to expose yourself; to have a direct no, or to be refused, and the door may be forever closed. Having the door closed too often can weaken the ally's relationship, the formed trust. As such, the efficient manager only uses this when he is guaranteed to succeed.

Indirect Influence

In indirect influence, you go through hoops and loops to make the target act and decide, while you remain in the background with the target being unaware that you are pulling the strings. There are many potential scenarios, with various degrees of success, depending on situations.

1. Common Ally

In this scenario, your ally is also an ally to the target. You need to work with your ally so that they perceive the value for themselves, in having the decision taken. They need someone to put keywords in their mouths so that they can relay why this decision is beneficial for the target as well. As this is a first level of difficulty, controlling the message can be done quite easily.

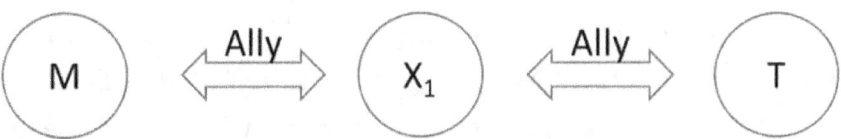

Figure 10: Indirect influence via a common ally

This method is safe, and if done properly you can easily control the outcome.

2. Common Ally, Plus Direct Access

Probably the most powerful method, when you combine the direct mentioned above and the first indirect method:

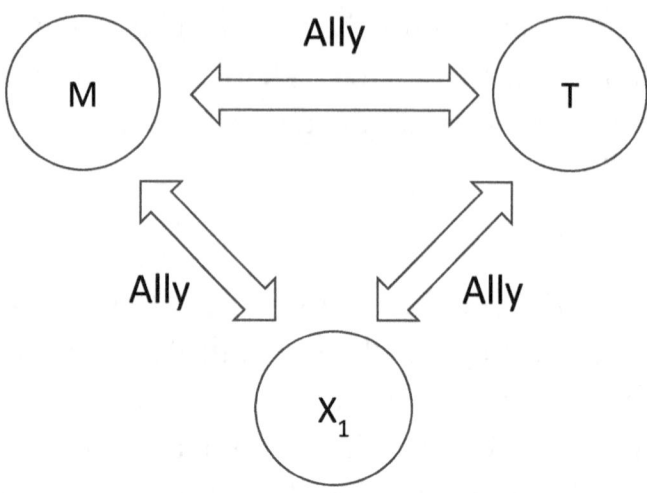

Figure 11: Hybrid direct and indirect influence

To avoid the risk implied in the direct approach, you only plant a seed. You insinuate informally the benefit, the general concept to the target, and in the background, you work directly with the common ally. When they do as asked with the message controlled, there will already be an openness, a fertile ground.

3. Longer Links – Two Degrees

Here, things need to be managed with more finesse. The idea is that your ally conveys the message to another ally of the target. For this to work, your ally (X_1) needs to carry the message as if they are the one for whom the decision is critical. They need to become "the source," so that in your ally's mind, they see the situation as them having a common ally with the target.

Common Ally scenario

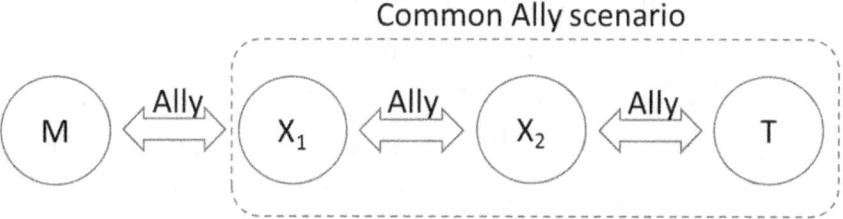

Figure 12: Indirect influence: longer links

If your ally, X_1, does not take the initiative to heart, the chain will be too weak and will fail. Preparation from the manager is paramount.

4. Longer Links – n Degrees

You can clearly see that with more than two degrees of freedom, this becomes very hard and improbable. The efficient manager does not waste efforts in highly improbable tactics. Speaking to only one ally and hoping that this goes well, meaning you control the situation through a chain of non-influenceable and uncontrollable relayers is a wasted effort. One tactic that can be used though is "triangulation." Launching a series of allies who each perceive the benefit from their perspective, who each are able to relay the message to one level closer, so that the message, even if weak, gets to the target from various sources. Repetition will eventually influence them.

This also can be used when you know something needs to happen, but you don't even know who the final target is. Launching several seeds, making sure they see the potential from their point of view or their finality, and putting control measures. For example, rechecking a few days later, weeks later, to see if they conveyed the message, what feedback they received, if this or that could be done as well. Basically, keeping gentle pressure on the allies so that they convey the message with more precision.

The Power of Indirect

As we saw, there are various forms of indirect tactics, and in each of them, there was an initial direct, not necessarily to the target itself, but to an ally or "seed planting." Since with the indirect approach you remain the string puller, if one fails then there are always other paths, other allies and influences to be leveraged.

As such, this is why Sun Tzu concludes on this topic by saying, "In battle, there are not more than two methods of attack – the direct and the indirect; yet these two in combination give rise to an endless series of maneuvers.[156] Indirect tactics, efficiently applied, are inexhaustible as Heaven and Earth, unending as the flow of rivers and streams; like the sun and moon, they end but to begin anew; like the four seasons, they pass away to return once more.[157]"

---

156 Translation from Lionel Giles, Chapter V, line 10
157 Translation from Lionel Giles, Chapter V, line 6

CHAPTER 40

MANAGING YOUR OWN STRENGTHS

HOW ONE MANAGES SPELLS out how others will follow and contribute, and you manage according to the values that you embody. If you have been reading most of the chapters up to now, you may realize that the number of capabilities, qualities, and strengths to be that "ultimate efficient manager" are endless: Which to nurture first, which is of prime importance, where to start?

I like to start with Sun Tzu's *The Art of War*, where his general represents today's manager: "The Commander stands for the virtues of wisdom, sincerely, benevolence, courage and strictness."[158]

The 5 Virtues

1. **Wisdom:** Understand the reality and the "how" to exploit the potential of the situation. Often our reading of a situation can be clouded by emotions, fear,

---

158 Translation from Lionel Giles, Chapter I, line 9

anger, lust, pride, and so on. The wise and strategic manager ponders and thinks through everything they see, and this can easily be learned by practicing taking a step back and taking a few deep breaths. Emotions typically last a very short time. In fact, according to Harvard brain scientist Dr. Jill Bolte Taylor,[159] 90 seconds is all it takes to identify an emotion and allow it to dissipate, while you simply notice it. So, step back, breathe for 90 seconds, clear your mind, and decide. In other words, wisdom is knowing the right thing to do. Furthermore, to be wise is to not constantly seek to impress others with one's wisdom; it is to speak with the words that are necessary. In a broader sense, it can refer to a manager's capability, competence to respond quickly to changes, and to anticipate the evolution of the situation and take advantage of it.

2. **Sincerity**: Believe in your approach and in what you do, be sincere toward yourself and the values you are nurturing. If you have doubts, it is often because your understanding of the context is not complete. These doubts can make you hesitate, and this will be seen by others, allies or not. Doubts are one of the five mental hindrances.[160] To be sincere is not to reveal all of your secrets, but to be truthful with what you say. Sincerity leads to trust: Can you, as a manager, be trusted? If a manager does not do what they say, their trust is

---

159 https://www.alysonmstone.com/90-seconds-to-emotional-resilience/
160 Chapter 27

questioned, and their team and allies may not follow them any longer.

3. **Benevolence:** Like compassion, help those you could hinder or harm in order to create new allies. Always have a reaching hand, show empathy. Allies are much fewer than strangers, so every time you can add one to your list, as a manager you will benefit. To be benevolent is not to be soft; it is to act in the best interests of others in the long run, rather than for short-term gain. The manager needs to love and protect their team, colleagues, allies, and the people working under them. It also means to treat people with respect and kindness, thereby winning the hearts of their followers. A manager who has their own self-interest as a priority will eventually fall. When you and your team win a certain project, reward your team with the recognition and incentives they deserve.

4. **Courage:** Go beyond your fears. This does not mean being reckless, it means discarding useless fears and hesitations to be able to take advantage of critical situations. It means standing up for your team and showing them that, as their manager, if something wrong happens you will take the blame since the team is your responsibility. A manager requires courage to make quick and difficult decisions. It is important to note that often a manager's valor is thought to be crucial in inspiring the entire army and lifting up its spirits. It reminds me of Winston Churchill's stirring speech to

the House of Commons in World War II: "We shall go on to the end. We shall fight in France, we shall fight on the seas and oceans, we shall fight with growing confidence and growing strength in the air, we shall defend our island, whatever the cost may be. We shall fight on the beaches, we shall fight on the landing grounds, we shall fight in the fields and in the streets, we shall fight in the hills; we shall never surrender."[161]

5. **Strictness:** Sincerity means, as highlighted above, making sure you do what you mean to do. Strictness is making sure when people commit to things like you, the cause, the team, they follow through and do it. To be strict does not mean being cruel, of course, it means ensuring that your instructions and commitments are obeyed for the organization to function efficiently. In a broader sense, it can mean having high standards for your team and having the determination to preserve them.

Having an obvious lack in these virtues is not a guarantee of failure, but it will certainly make strategy implementation and management more difficult. Spending time and energy cultivating and harvesting their team transforms a boss into a leader and a true, dynamic, and efficient manager.

---

161 https://winstonchurchill.org/resources/speeches/1940-the-finest-hour/we-shall-fight-on-the-beaches/

CHAPTER 41

MANAGING COHERENCE

WE HAVE DISCUSSED A lot about helping your teams, colleagues, and allies by using compassion, altruism, and coaching. All this is great, but as highlighted in a Harvard Business Review article, "To take care of others, start by taking care of yourself."[162]

We have discussed the importance of managers, and further studies show that a staggering 94 percent of employees who like their boss are passionate about their jobs,[163] whereas 77 percent of people who do not like their boss hope to leave their job soon.[164] How can employees feel great about their boss if the boss or the manager does not feel great about themself?

Always Improve

We are quick to judge others, thinking, "They should have done this," "I wish they could do that," "I would

162 https://hbr.org/2020/04/to-take-care-of-others-start-by-taking-care-of-yourself

163 https://www.predictiveindex.com/learn/inspire/resources/surveys-reports/people-man-agement-survey-2018/

164 https://www.betterup.com/blog/awakening-human-potential-and-driving-performance-work

have done things differently ..." But who really takes the time to analyze oneself, to reflect on their own actions, inactions, and reactions to see if they were appropriate, to understand where they came from, to see if they brought you closer to the ideal that you set for yourself, or even just to reflect on what is that ideal you have for yourself? I see many managers just being who they are because that is what they are. There are several ways to go about reflecting on oneself such as journaling, hiring a coach, meditating, reflecting on your day, your week, and so on. The point is, we should always, as managers, try to improve ourselves. But sometimes it is hard to make that self-assessment, and if done, it is hard to know where to start. So many things could be improved, so we either get discouraged and rely on the status quo or try to solve everything at once and fail.

A powerful way to do this as a manager, which can also be applied to other aspects of life, is with a wheel of values or a radar chart, often known as a spider web diagram.[165]

Put six to 10 managerial dimensions on your diagram, and give yourself a grade, an appreciation mark. As an example:

You can either do this for general managerial skills or pinpoint a certain situation, such as a particular managerial scenario where you would like to improve.

---

165 https://www.tibco.com/reference-center/what-is-a-radar-chart

Figure 13: Managerial radar chart example

Once the wheel is completed, it is easy to see where you need special attention. In this example, stress management and work happiness level. You are not a collaborative manager, a Zen manager, or a happy one. Try to find the main stress contributor and address it. This is often what we can call a keystone behavior. By addressing a main aspect of the behavior, it can have repercussions on others. Tackling your main stress contribution in this example can help reduce overall stress, giving you better tools to manage other stressful situations, and by the same ripple effect increase your work happiness level.

This quote from Lao Tzu sums it up quite well: "Knowing others is intelligence but knowing yourself is true wisdom."[166]

Coherence Leading to Being Credible

In the example above, the manager was neither Zen nor happy at work. Regardless of how good an actor you are, people, subordinates, and allies will realize it. How can you ask them to be relaxed? How can you complain or be surprised when they leave, or burn out, when they are stressed and unhappy? We all can relate to the image of an overweight, smoking doctor trying to convince his patients to lose weight and stop smoking in order to improve their health. At some point, yes, the doctor in question has the knowledge, but does he have the credibility to be convincing on those particular topics? The same is true in the managerial world. This lack of coherence between what is said and what is transmitted in the messages sent by actions and reactions is made daily. Here are some examples:

- You ask your team to free up some time to work on something else, yet your own agenda is overfilled.
- You ask your team to deliver on time, yet you are always late for meetings.
- You ask your team to have a positive attitude, yet you are grumpy.

---

166 Tao Te Ching, Chapter 33, translation by Stephen Mitchell

• You ask your team to focus, yet you go on and on and get distracted.

A fellow by the name of Albert Einstein once said, "Setting an example is not the main means of influencing others, it is the only means."[167] Both this quote and these examples demonstrate how hard it is to be a good English teacher if your own English sucks, how hard it is to be a good financial counselor if you go bankrupt, and how hard it is to be a good manager if you can't manage yourself. In his book *Freedom for All of Us*, Matthieu Ricard tells a story from the sage Mulla Nasrudin[168] in which a mother brought her child to see him. She asks the sage to tell the child to stop eating candies and cookies, hoping the authority of Nasrudin would be more influential than her own. Nasrudin told the mother to come back in 15 days. At the end of this period, the mother came back, and Nasrudin told the kid while looking him straight in the eyes to stop eating such food. Impressed, the child nodded. Curious, the mother asked Nasrudin why they had to wait 15 days, to which the sage answered, "I needed to validate for myself that such a task was possible."

Speaking of coherence, when the Dalai Lama was asked what surprised him most about humanity, he answered: "Man! Because he sacrifices his health in order to make money. Then he sacrifices money to recuperate his health.

---

167 Goodreads.com, Albert Einstein Quotes
168 https://www.allaboutturkey.com/nasreddin.html

And then he is so anxious about the future that he does not enjoy the present; the result being that he does not live in the present or the future; he lives as if he is never going to die, and then dies having never really lived."[169] Try to be coherent as a manager, and to achieve this, know yourself and always improve.

CHAPTER 42

MANAGING LIKE PETER PAN

IN THE CLASSIC MOVIE *Hook,*[170] Robin Williams plays an old Peter Pan who has forgotten who he used to be. Peter Banning is now an unimaginative and workaholic lawyer. When Captain Hook comes to London to steal his kids, Banning needs to go back to Neverland and save them, but he can only do so as Peter Pan, not Peter Banning. In one of the key scenes, a Lost Boy twists Williams' face back and forth and at some point, the Lost Boy brightens up and declares: "Oh, there you are, Peter!"

The question is now, where is YOUR Peter Pan?

The True Nature

As Lao Tzu puts it, "It is the child that sees the primordial secret of Nature and it is the child of ourselves we return to, the child within us is simple and daring enough to live the Secret."[171]

---

170 https://www.imdb.com/title/tt0102057/
171 Goodreads.com, Lao Tzu Quotes

Children are innocent. They have not seen and lived the impacts of adulthood for the most part. They have no filters, they see with amazement and a new set of eyes, every experience creating new synapses in their flourishing mind. They think and speak often without a filter. They represent, to some extent, the true nature of self.

The adult that you are now, was once that child: an innocent, amazed, discovering, unfiltered, and unbiased child. You had the world at your fingertips. Yet life has shaped you, with "don't do this," "do that," "don't touch," "don't," "don't," "do," "do." With this molding, and some unconscious yet self-imposed limitations and habits, there often follows stress, anxiety, frustrations, and a plethora of negative emotions.

But what if …? What if you tried to get back to parts of what made you a child, parts of that primordial secret and parts of that fundamental essence that makes you, you?

The exercise is simple. Find a few photographs of yourself when you were in your single-digit years and name a few qualities you see in the child you are looking at on those pictures. What would some of those be? Playful? Happy? Cheerful? Dynamic? Entertaining? Zen? Creative? Imaginative? Resilient? Curious? Adaptable? Confident? Now ask yourself how would my adult life be if I embodied a couple of those qualities and behaviors that were at the core of who I was born to be? How would they impact my managerial life?

The Gap

Because of the social pressures and life's work on us, we often drift from those, we grow up and "become adult." The gap between what we were, our core essence, and who we become, forged by circumstances, widens. However, I would argue that when you do what you love, your passion becomes obvious and the quality of what you "produce" explodes. Work is a hobby, not a daunting task to do in order to survive and put food on the table. This passion is contagious. It energizes people around you, encourages them to look for their passion, to become what they could be. This is the seed of inspirational leadership. Leadership does not necessarily mean being upfront with inflammatory speeches like Captain America; leaders offer the inspiration that motivates us to do more, to do better, with a positive attitude.

The fundamental idea is to bridge the gap between who you are and what you do. The more you can do that, the happier you will be and the more successful a manager you will become. And one of the best ways to find out who you are is to go back to who you were before "life" happened to find your Peter Pan.

Unconditional Peter

You know what they say about how parents feel toward their children...unconditional love. Unconditional. There are obviously certain exceptions, but for the vast majority, I believe it to be true. Your children are a part of you,

you are a part of them. That bond creates that unconditional love, even expanding the circle to nieces, nephews, and children of your best friend. As Matthieu Ricard says: "We all have unconditional love for a child."[172]

Of course, the closer the child, the more natural and easier the feeling, hence our children.

But there is one other child even closer to us than our kids. Take a look again at that photograph of you as a child that we discussed earlier on. How about THAT child? Can you feel unconditional love for them?

Many of us as adults have forgotten that, just like we have forgotten our inner Peter Pan. Instead of internally judging ourselves, complaining about whatever we didn't do right or what we missed or what we did not achieve to the perfection that we believe we can, why don't we take the time for self-compassion, self-appreciation of what was accomplished and self-love? Unconditional self-love?

This changes everything. Suddenly you are more luminous, more radiant, and more content. You are impacting your life, and this energy is contagious; it is inspiring. This is what great efficiency is all about as a manager.

Find your Peter Pan, and ask yourself, what would he tell the adult that you've become? He would tell you to nurture that unconditional love for that great child who was and who still is. Start flying, with or without pixie dust.

---

172 https://www.businessinsider.com/matthieu-ricard-tibetan-buddhist-monk-happiest-man-2017-12

CHAPTER 43

MANAGING HUMANITY

AS MANAGERS, WE DEAL with people either under our supervision or not, but people, nonetheless. To reuse the quote from Sun Tzu that I used in Chapter 28, "Regard your soldiers as your children, and they will follow you into the deepest valleys; look upon them as your own beloved sons, and they will stand by you even unto death." How do we bring that humanity to the managerial table to help us gain efficiency?

The Boss vs. the Coach

Most managers are either promoted nonmanagers or entrepreneurs and have had little, if any, managerial training. I have discussed this at length in a previous chapter.[173] As such, there is a tendency to adopt the "boss" persona. The typical state of mind, shall I say obsession, of this persona is result-oriented, actionable results, for them, for their group.

Part of the "boss" persona also comes from the perceived operational "job" of the boss, the one that is

---

173 Chapter 25

more visible, more often noticed and appreciated by external eyes, such as doing reports, achieving KPIs, solving issues, and so on. Going through this to-do list is seen as mandatory, especially for the new boss, and it is often easier, reassuring, and gives the feeling of "doing their job."

In the same manner, some people are often seen with typical behaviors of the "boss" persona. They may be in the line of someone who:

- Speaks, directs, and is task-oriented
- Has authority and provides answers
- Sets goals and tells what to do
- Looks for predictable results
- Uses constraints to reduce goals
- Makes hot issues hard to discuss
- Looks for what's wrong and why problems happen
- Walks the quick route to deal with surface symptoms

Not much humanity in there, though. On the other hand, if we talk about a coach, their typical state of mind, or obsession, is the growth of the other, not their own, not their own results. In contrast with the "boss" persona, here are some typical behaviors of the coach persona, someone who:

- Listens, inspires, and empowers for growth
- Partners and provides questions
- Listens then links to organizational needs

- Engages in creating impossible futures
- Looks for unprecedented results
- Uses constraints to spark breakthroughs
- Discusses the undiscussable
- Looks for what's missing, which if provided can make a difference
- Uncovers issues to get to the root cause

Much more human, but not really short-term results oriented.

Actionable results vs. gradual transformation: The challenge of the manager is to weave one within the other. To become obsessed not with results, not with the other, but with **how the development and the growth of the other can contribute, help, and enable the achievement of the results.**

Maybe the best way to show how this can be done is through examples.

New Skill Example

Let's say that, as a manager, you would like one of your employees to show more initiative, take the lead and take more risks.

The boss approach could be to use the yearly or mid-year appraisal, and give him/her an objective: "I would like you to show more initiative this year. This would help the team in such and such way or would help me." "Since we need to do SMART objectives,[174] I want you to propose five initiatives in the next three months…"

Now not too sure of the why and the how, the employee will try and document five different things, just to get the thumbs-up and the good grade, never to learn or grow in the process.

The efficient human/coach approach would be to ask the employee what dreams and visions they have for themself, how they see their growth and development within the company, not necessarily within the team. Show interest in whatever they say, ask questions such as "Why?" or "How can I, as your manager, help you?" etc. At some point, ask them what skills they think they would need to get where they want to go. If taking initiative is not one of them, the manager can suggest, "What about taking more initiative? I believe that in future roles it would be a great asset. If I were to hire you, that is something I would be looking for …" Then followed by, "What type of initiatives? How can I support you? Shall we do a monthly progression session?"

The employee feels heard, empowered, supported, and coached, and will grow more rapidly.

Failure Example

In this scenario, the employee comes and tells you that a project is late or that they failed to achieve the objectives of their task.

---

174 Chapter 30

The boss's approach could be to show some level of disappointment, saying for example, "Why am I learning of this now? The impacts of this on the business are such and such," or the famous "This is unacceptable."

The efficient human/coach approach could be to realize that what is done is done, and their first words could be, "Thank you for your honesty and your trust, it means a lot." Notice the positivity versus the first answer. The conversation can then easily evolve in the direction of, "What did you learn in the process? Do you know where the wheels came off the wagon? What would be one step, change, you can bring into your work to help mitigate and avoid this happening in the future? I suggest we do a follow-up in a few weeks to see how you have implemented that first step, if you feel it is anchored solidly enough, and if so, then what could be another step? Oh, and by the way, when do you think you can deliver the project?"

Again, the employee feels heard, empowered, supported, and coached, and will grow more rapidly.

Wrap-up

In both cases, the result will be achieved, so the "boss" persona can be satisfied, but it will affect the growth of the employee. Imagine how that employee will behave moving forward.

Even though in my definition of a manager,[175] the word "resource" is present, never forget that they are humans. Use them as resources, but most importantly, treat them as living beings.

Could this be called "silent leadership"?

---

[175] Chapter 1

CHAPTER 44

MANAGING THE ORG CHART

THE ORGANIZATIONAL CHART,[176] or org chart for short, as previously discussed, outlines the roles of the various "levels" as individual levels.[177] Now, let's take a look at the entire chart from an efficient manager's point of view and find things that no one else sees, giving us the edge for efficiency.

The Top Down

Look at any company's org chart. Regardless of how "flat" the company is attempting to make its organization, the org chart always looks like some kind of pyramid. The CEO on the top, fewer executives going down, and a high number of executants at the base. Often the salaries also follow that hierarchy.

---

176 https://www.lucidchart.com/pages/tutorial/organizational-charts
177 Chapter 25

Figure 14: Typical top-down org chart

As discussed,[178] the levels on top often believe they are smarter, more important, and have a free pass to delegate, use authority, and sometimes be condescending because they are "on top."

Of course, the CEO is often the one with the visions of grandeur; they see where they want to be heading, see the opportunities, etc. Sometimes they are the one who created the enterprise. They are important in the organization. But as we know from the Tower of Pisa,[179] a strong foundation is critically important for maintaining a structure, such as an org chart pyramid. Any construction, now or at the beginning, is built from the ground up, not from the top down. Let's explore that idea.

---

178 Chapter 28
179 https://www.towerofpisa.org/

From the Ground Up

The importance of having a foundation cannot be over-stated. In the org chart pyramid, the foundation is made out of people doing the products, delivering the services, selling the solutions, fixing problems, hiring new parts of the foundation, and so forth.

All the layers in between, from VPs to directors to managers, all have their importance, but a significant chunk of their roles is to organize the work, to opti-mize the flow, and to manage the output of the teams below them; in other terms, the managing of the foun-dation. Of course, it is not only that, but if one were to ask, what would be the answer? In the org chart shown above, which layer if removed would have the least impact? Once that layer is removed, then which one would be next? Continue the questioning until there are only two layers left. Which would be those two lay-ers? Likely this:

Figure 15: Minimalistic top-down org chart

This is the bare minimum.

The Forgotten Layer

In the Chapter on the three corporate entities,[180] we defined:

- The financer: Of the two layers left, the top layer takes care of this entity
- The makers: The other remaining layer
- The buyers: Where are they in the chart?

Any company that wants to grow, prosper, survive, and live, needs customers to buy their goods and services. The truth is, they are the most important layer. You can have a great CEO and great workers that make fantastic products and offer amazing services. But if nobody is willing to pay for them, nothing else matters. Where is this layer in the org chart? Where are the customers, the most important entities in the viability and sustainability of the enterprise?

They are simply not there.

Typically, in all the layers of the initial org chart, which one interacts the most with customers? It would be the individual salesperson, the technical support, the engineers, and the marketing people. They are the ones interacting with the most important entity and yet they are at the bottom of the chart and this entity, the customers, are absent from the org chart.

---

180 Chapter 11

Who should be supporting these "front-line workers"? Their managers, their supervisors, their directors, the C-suite ...

Should the value and importance org chart look more like this?

Figure 16: Customer-centric org chart

The Efficient Manager

Of course, few companies would ever display their org chart like this, out of tradition, habit, and a strong ego needing to be on the top. But as efficient managers, never neglect this concept and make sure your values, your strategies, and your network are optimized to achieve your goals and finality.

As Sun Tzu states: "A victorious general wins first and then goes to war while a defeated one goes to war and then seeks to win."[181] To be the first winner, know your army, who is important, who fights in the trenches every day to make a difference, whether in your team or not. Make sure they are ready for the battle and they, directly or not, serve your finality.

---

181 Translation from Lionel Giles, Chapter IV, line 15

CHAPTER 45

MANAGING PROCRASTINATION

PROCRASTINATION CAN BE DEFINED as the art of avoiding necessary tasks and instead shifting the focus to more pleasant and satisfying ones. We've all been there, pushing that report, that presentation aside and doing something else instead.

According to Piers Steel, about 95 percent of people admit to putting off work,[182] so it's safe to assume most of us are procrastinators at times.

Procrastination does not mean laziness; it is just pushing back what needs to be done. In fact, procrastination finds its roots in our biology, just like habit creation. It's the result of a constant battle in our brain between the limbic system and the prefrontal cortex.

The Battle

In Plato's *Protagoras*,[183] Socrates asks how it is possible that if one judges an action to be the best, one would

---

182 https://procrastinus.com/piers-steel/purchase-the-procrastination-equation/
183 http://classics.mit.edu/Plato/protagoras.html

do anything other than this action. In other words, why are we procrastinating? Let's review the battleground a bit:

- **Limbic system** : one of the oldest and most dominant portions of the brain. Its processes are mostly automatic. When you are in the flight-or-fight mode, it's your limbic system taking over. This reactive, primal part of the brain is looking to stay safe, and once safe, is looking for instant gratification (the dopamine response). All animals have one.
- **Prefrontal cortex** : a newer, less developed, and as a result somewhat weaker portion of the brain. This is the part of your brain where planning, looking ahead, and making decisions happens. The prefrontal cortex is the part of the brain that separates humans from animals.

So, to answer Socrates's question, it is because the limbic system is much stronger, it very often wins the battle, which leads to procrastination. When there is no danger, no trigger of the flight-or-fight system, we, by default, give our brain what feels good *now*, instant gratification (look at young children, for example).

To explain it plainly, the mind compares two tasks, the one that will save us or bring instant gratification (like having fun), versus the mundane one that needs to eventually be done. Without will and mindfulness, it will often choose the instant-gratification route.

The Why Cycle

In addition to the reasons listed above, there are some-times strong motivations to avoid the important task, which pushes us on the path of procrastination. Some people procrastinate out of fear of being judged for their work, so they just avoid completing the task. Others are thrill-seekers who claim to enjoy the rush that comes with racing to meet a deadline. There are, of course, a vast array of other potential reasons. To name only a few:

- Fear of failure
- Stress
- Avoiding bad emotions, bad feelings
- Subconscious mind – thinking the task is useless
- Mental health – depression, bad mood, mood swings
- Self-regulation issues – being used to a world of instant grat-ification, instant everything
- Disliking the task

It is a common misconception that procrastination is due to a problem with managing time, when, in fact, it is a much more complex issue. Our mood and attitude toward the task and ourselves determine our level of procrasti-nation. We act based on our beliefs, and, in turn, those actions continuously shape those beliefs. It is a cycle, here again, that leads eventually to our self-identity.

As managers, we need to give our prefrontal cortex a little help in fighting the good fight against our lazy, self-indulgent limbic system. The cycle needs to be weakened to gain efficiency. But how?

Deadlines

Now we can separate procrastination into two big buckets...the tasks that have deadlines and those that don't.

- **Deadline tasks:** While we procrastinate here, we know a deadline will come. When the deadline approaches, another part of the limbic system kicks in...the fear of failure, the lack of safety...the stress similar to the flight-and-fight response. So, when this kicks in, then we get to it. There is often an adrenaline rush, and we often manage to eventually get it in on time. Yet we did not evolve from animals to be constantly pursued by lions and tigers...living under this constant stress, while helping us to achieve, is biologically quite bad for us.

- **Non-deadline tasks:** In this case, this last-minute panic never happens, we never "do it" based on the survival instinct of the limbic system. There is no momentum, no "start or end," no fight and flight, last-minute survival, and so nothing ever gets done, nothing ever gets started...This may lead to longer-term negative emotions, unhappiness, and regrets. It makes you feel like a spectator in your own life, you don't even start chasing whatever dream you have. We need to short-circuit it, we need to willingly break the cycle and, as Nike says, "Just do it."

Motivation

One of the ways to achieve this cycle break is, of course, through willpower. But just like muscle power, willpower does not happen overnight. There are mental fitness exercises, and practices, to grow it, to build that willingness to travel that path away from the voices trying to sabotage us, and down the path of self-realization.

Every pleasant experience releases dopamine. The instant gratification is a reason as mentioned above why the limbic system often wins. So, one of the keys to counteracting this cycle is by creating instant-gratification elements in the planning, in the daunting and longer tasks. Changing perspectives about the activity is a good trick, changing its context or focusing on the bright side of the task. Breaking it into smaller tasks with a reward system at the end of each part is also a great motivation as is changing your environment to have fewer distractions and temptations or simply changing it to stay alert. When there are no deadlines (for example, eating better or getting in better shape), you can either create one yourself by making a commitment/contract with yourself or try to start a habit until it becomes natural. As I've said before, habits lead to character, and character defines your personality. So, with a bit of willpower, technique, and time, procrastination can lead to new efficient habits.

CHAPTER 46

MANAGING PRIORITIES

EVERYTHING SEEMS URGENT; EVERYTHING needs to be done yesterday or the day before. Days are endless, the candle is burning at both ends. Now what? Managing priorities seems simple to say, but everything seems to be a top priority. Does that mean back to square one?

Important vs. Urgent

There is a simple model that is well-known: divide or label your tasks according to importance and urgency. It is called the Eisenhower Decision Matrix.[184]

Urgent tasks are those that cause us to react; we stop what we are doing and need to work on that specific task, if not now, then soon since the window of opportunity will close. These tasks have tight deadlines. On the other hand, important tasks lead toward our goals, our finality. Since these goals are important to reach, they require planning and initiative. As US President Eisenhower said in a

---

184 https://www.eisenhower.me/eisenhower-matrix/

speech, quoting Dr. J. Roscoe Miller: "What is important is seldom urgent and what is urgent is seldom important."[185]

Table 3: Eisenhower Decision Matrix

1- Urgent and Important	2- Not urgent and Important
3- Not important but Urgent	4- Not important and Not Urgent

Of course, for a lot of people, both words mean the same thing. Or for someone else, they push back the important (see the chapter on procrastination[186]) until they become urgent.

The urgency should be easy to figure out. Is there a very near deadline associated with the task and is the magnitude of the task making it a challenge to achieve that deadline? If you answer yes to both, then the task is urgent. But one big question remains: how do you determine if any given activity is important or not, regardless of its urgency?

In the chapter about time management,[187] I discussed the famous to-do list or the importance of achieving versus doing, in other words, what you achieved as opposed to what you did. If the task has a typical "to-do list" set of characteristics like a start and an end, it is binary (done versus not done). While it may appear important, these characteristics may be misleading. To go a step further in

185 https://www.mindtools.com/pages/article/newHTE_91.htm#:~:text=Eisenhower%2C%20who%20was%20quoting%20Dr,organized%20his%20workload%20and%20priorities.
186 Chapter 45
187 Chapter 15

determining its real importance, let's revisit the chapter about managing finality,[188] where I take a deep dive into what a finality **is**, how it is driven by the corporate finalities of viability and sustainability, and how those are trickled down to your function, your group, and yourself.

In truth, the task is seldom important. One needs to answer: **Is** that task or activity helping me achieve something in regard to my finality? Is it making me progress in that direction? If so, how? And how do I need to tweak the task to optimize the achievement on that finality continuum? A finality is not binary like a goal, we can always improve, and draw closer to it. If you never figured out your finality, then you are back to evaluating the task for its binary essence.

In other words, how does it serve your finality? If it doesn't, it is not important regardless of what may be perceived. If it does, then it has the potential **to** be important. This is where you need to weigh the ratio of how much it **is** helping your finality versus the effort you will put into it. What is that ratio? And can the ratio be improved in any way if I decide to do it? Or can **you** progress faster with less risk and effort along **your** finality axis by doing something else instead?

As such, while the question "Is it urgent?" may have a clear yes/no answer based on the deadline (in the binary, operational, non-managerial world), the question "Is it

---

188 Chapter 22

important?" has a more nuanced answer. I would argue that finding out that answer for many activities is an important task as it can drastically change your agenda and your progress toward your finality.

The Quadrants

Elements in quadrant 1 appear in a crisis environment. They come out of nowhere and are unforeseen (if they had been expected, they would not be urgent). They often show a lack of understanding of global reality, pointing out something we missed, had not anticipated or had not prepared for. These shouldn't appear too often if you follow what I explained in the chapter about managing difficulties.[189] Since urgent things require immediate action, it's best to always be as prepared as possible to avoid tasks occurring in this quadrant, and if they do, to deal with them as swiftly as possible. These urgent tasks are often binary and nonmanagerial, and so have little managerial added value. This is the anti-Zen quadrant ... deadlines and panics. They are not the mark of efficient managers.

Items in quadrant 3, the urgent yet not important, are often interruptions. They may be important for someone else, and they relay that importance to you, yet they do not feed into your finality. Every interruption chews away some time, and efficient managers are great at managing time.

---

189 Chapter 36

Items in quadrant 4, not important and not urgent, are distractions. They may be fun, and the instant gratification part of our brain may love them, but these, just as tasks from quadrant 3, need to be turned refused. These tasks should not even be delegated to members of your team since these people help you achieve your finality as well. On the other hand, if, for example, these tasks help you create a strong ally, these may shift from a not-important task to an important one. The importance would not be in the activity itself but in the accomplishment. In this case, creating an ally who can and will be useful down the road.

This leaves quadrant 2, the important yet not urgent. As mentioned above, importance is relative, there are lots of shades of importance. However, those activities that make their way to this quadrant are there because they help you achieve something greater and larger than only doing the task. They move needles, they plant seeds, they prepare an eventual move, and so on.

These activities are the ones the efficient manager must focus on, using everything they've learned so far: riding the wave, direct and indirect influence, allies, and spies, and the like. The more things are foreseen, planned, and optimized here, the more you will cruise toward your finality.

You will spend less effort while doing so because your achievements will flow naturally by riding the wave of whatever unfolds and steers it to where you need to go. This is the Zen, all under control, easygoing, "look at me" quadrant. It is the "look at me because I seem not to do much, but everything always falls into place" quadrant.

This is why it is important to take some time to figure out what is important and why. Planning importance is the only guaranteed important task efficient managers have, and it is most often neglected.

CHAPTER 47

MANAGING DELEGATION

TO DELEGATE MEANS TO entrust a task or responsibility to another person, typically one who is in a less senior position than you. As a manager, we often believe we need to delegate more, that this, for example, is a good way to teach others how to do a certain job that we could do and/or for selfish reasons to try to free up our agenda a little bit. Yet there are many reasons, conscious or not, why we don't delegate.

So, to delegate is to ask someone to do a certain job. It refers to the transfer of responsibility for specific tasks from one person to another. As their boss, as their manager, you are naturally entitled to do that. Let's look at delegation from the efficient manager's point of view.

Why Not?

There are many reasons why many managers have a hard time delegating, some of them for example being:

- **Thinks it would take longer to explain the task than completing it themself**.[190]

---

190 Chapter 32

- o "I'm the manager, I should be better." How can you ever build and grow a team, how can you ever take control of your agenda with this attitude?
- **Enjoys completing certain projects, so prefers not to reassign them**
  - o As a manager, you have roles and responsibilities; if you prefer operational tasks, maybe management is not your thing.
- **Feels guilty about adding more work to another employee's to-do list**
  - o We have discussed to-do lists in previous chapters. Coaching, empowering, and prioritization based on accomplishments versus activities can be used to avoid this issue.
- **Lack confidence or trust in whom they need to transfer the project to**
  - o If you do not trust or have confidence in your team, ask yourself why. It is the manager's role to make sure his team grows, that they are competent. Delegation gives a chance to make sure the others learn and that you can have a silver lining to help them evolve in the direction that will serve you and the employee.
- **Believe that they're the only ones who can do the job right**
  - o Similar to the previous point, plus this will guarantee that you are always overwhelmed and overworked, the opposite of efficiency.

Inflexion Point

In the chapter about ultimate efficiency,[191] we discussed how to make sure what needed to be done was in the natural evolution of things; plant the seed and, if watered and cared for, it will grow into whatever was coded in the seed. Hard delegation can be seen like planting a tomato seed, and after a few weeks, realizing you need cucumbers and forcing the tomato plant to produce cucumbers.

Your employees, teams, and resources all have their reality based on their jobs, mandates, and perceptions of what they need to do. Their agenda is planned; they have to deliver, to accomplish things. They are on a set course.

When you arrive with a new task, via delegation, you create an inflexion point, and change the direction of the course, abruptly, directly, without much choice since you are the boss.

As with everything, when you create an inflection point, there is force applied, there is a risk of breaking, and there is another reality that won't happen. There is a specific point in time where the path changed. Therefore, there is a risk in delegating and the various reasons mentioned above are why people may be afraid of delegating.

In Reality

Naturally, you cannot do all the tasks yourself, that is beyond inefficient. However, pure delegation may not be

---

191 Chapter 17

the best solution because of that force applied directly to a situation with the risks implied. Let's look at these different scenarios, assuming you know that whatever you would like to delegate, Bob is the best to take it on:

- Bob, please do this task ...
- Bob, can you please take care of this task?

These two formulations are delegation-oriented (you can add gravy, context, etc., but ultimately you are asking Bob directly to do it).

Another formulation, after giving some context as to why and what, is:

- Bob, when could this task be completed?

Without asking, you imply that Bob will do it. It is a veiled delegation. For some, this more subtle way can be ideal, for others, it may seem more dictatorial. Now consider this last option after giving context of what and why the task should be done:

- Team, you see the importance, who wants to tackle this? Whom do you feel should take care of this?

And if it is obvious this is a task for Bob, someone will suggest him, or he will suggest himself. If another name comes up, you can decide if you are okay with this other name or answer something like, "Thanks for the suggestion, I was thinking maybe Bob. What do you all think?"

This still remains a team decision and you offer help, assistance, guidance, and checkpoints.

In such a scenario, there is no direct force applied, no inflexion point; Bob's reality line shifts direction, but by his own doing, his own decision, and he does not perceive it as a delegation, just part of what he would normally do. Or if his name is suggested by peers, it is flattering and anything but a delegation. This is much smoother.

As Sun Tzu mentions in his chapter about force, "Getting people to fight by letting the force of momentum work is like rolling logs and rocks. Logs and rocks are still when in a secure place but roll on an incline, they remain stationary if square, they roll if round."[192]

Delegation is like pushing a log on a flat surface. The manager creates the incline, and the rest will happen naturally. No breaks, no force, no risks. Try to shape water; the only way you will ever succeed is by shaping its environment. Shape the context and the tasks will get done naturally, no delegation required.

---

192 Translation from Lionel Giles, Chapter V, line 22

CHAPTER 48

MANAGING SPEECH

AS MANAGERS, WE OFTEN need to give advice, suggestions, and mandates. We need to help people grow, coach them, train them, and teach them. If we have direct reports, we need to evaluate them and make them become the best version of who they can become. So, managing speech is a critical aspect of the efficient manager's role to achieve those ambitions and results and not achieve the opposite: fear, stress, demotivation, and guilt.

Advice, suggestions, and mandates can all be given the right way or the wrong way.

So, how to speak "in the right way" to get whatever message across, understood, but in an uplifting way, regardless of the message? Let's explore a path taught to us by Buddhism. In his definition of the four noble truths,[193] the fourth one is *"The truth of the path that leads to the end of suffering."* That path has eight sections. We have discussed the first two at length in various other chapters: the right understanding and the right thoughts. The third one is the right speech, which can be well applied to the efficient manager.

193 https://www.britannica.com/topic/Four-Noble-Truths

The Right Speech – Time

Yes, we have often talked about a manager's perspective about time and time as a resource. But here, we will look at a different aspect of time: the right time.

Often, when something true needs to be said that can be helpful, it might not be easy for someone else to hear. In this case, we need to think carefully about when to say it. Some moments are better than others. Some moods of the people we are talking to are more favorable. When people are well rested and at peace, rather than stressed and agitated, for example, they respond better to a discussion. Sometimes it is better to bide your time and wait for a more appropriate time to speak to someone when the situation will allow it to flow more naturally. This brings us back the notion of water,[194] of fluidity and naturalism.

Finding the best time to say something might determine whether or not the words are beneficial. The same can be said for compliments. Sometimes the mind is open to receiving them, sometimes they just go in one ear and out the other, with no impact whatsoever. But just as there is a right time, there is also a wrong time. A wrong time will create resistance, which is the antithesis of efficiency.

Timing, therefore, plays a huge role in speech efficiency.

---

194 Chapter 5

The Right Speech – Place

The time may be good as well as the mood, the opportunity, and the potential openness, but the place may be wrong. If there is a right place to say what needs to be said, it means there is a wrong place. For example, when many people are around to tell a truth that may hurt a bit.

Place can mean the people around you; speaking truth in front of colleagues may hurt, even if the time seems good, the place may not be. Place can mean a physical location. For example, the boss's office is more intimidating, less prone to open conversation, than over lunch.

Together, time and space, and place create the condition and the situation.

The Right Speech – Words

I love this particular sentence from the Abbot of the Shaolin Temple Europe:[195] "Truth should be like a warm blanket around the shoulders, not like a wet blanket slapping your face."

There are four qualities to speech once the right time and right place are present.

- **Factual and true** It should not be a surprise to read that right speech is incompatible with lying. But factual and truth go beyond this…it is absent from opinion, from bias and perspective. What may be true to you is not necessarily true to

---

195 https://www.shaolintemple.eu/

others. A simple example is to state that the sky is blue, versus the sky is beautiful. A lot of time, managers and colleagues shape the reality with their roles, mandates, obligations, and experiences. This does not mean they are factual or true. Another example is if someone is impolite at the moment. While it may be true at the moment, it may not be factual. The fact is how you have perceived it.

- **Helpful, beneficial** We never know in advance, of course, but we should have good intentions, a feeling that what we will say will be useful or helpful.

- **Spoken with kindness and goodwill** This means hoping for the best for all involved. The Dalai Lama says, "Be kind whenever possible. Then adds, It is always possible."[196] Have good intentions when you speak. Do not belittle, diminish, ridicule, insult, or show off. The more goodwill you put in your intentions, the more the proper words will come out. You are concentrated on the needs and the situation of the other one, instead of your own. With this, you better your chances of being properly heard, accepted, and benefited. Do you have judgment or discernment (factual or perceptional)?

- **Endearing, or spoken gently** No yelling, shouting, or harsh intonations. Failing to consider how your words are going to make someone feel shows self-centeredness. Everybody likes to hear nice words; nobody likes to hear malicious ones.

---

196 Goodreads.com, Dalai Lama XIV Quotes

This is, as mentioned above in the context of wanting to help, how to make a fellow colleague grow and flourish. There are other types of speeches, like in negotiations when trying to have the upper hand, that were discussed briefly in the Fight, Flight, or Manage chapter,[197] when paraphrasing *The Treatise for Efficacy*.

The more professional the environment, the less we accept mistakes. Yet, they are part of us. Find compassion. Find respect. Find care. Talk in a way that people can keep their honor and save face. Both you and they will profit from the words, like a warm blanket around your shoulders.

---

197 Chapter 2

CHAPTER 49

MANAGING RHETORIC

IN THE PREVIOUS CHAPTER, we analyzed the right way to speak when the purpose is to make colleagues and employees grow or when giving mandates, suggestions, and corrections. We did mention that this type of speech was different from negotiations, or speech aimed at gaining an advantage in order to move a pawn in a better position for our finality. This is called rhetoric. The Cambridge Dictionary defines rhetoric as "The art of persuasion utilized by speakers to inform, persuade, or motivate a particular audience in specific situations."[198]

Many believe that the efficient use of rhetoric comes from the teachings of Plato and Aristotle in ancient Greece. The truth is a text from ancient China is now considered the earlier treatise devoted entirely to the art of rhetoric. This treatise is called the Guiguzi, and we briefly talked about it in the chapter about managing ignorance.[199]

So, let's explore Guiguzi from the perspective of an efficient manager.

---

198 https://dictionary.cambridge.org/dictionary/english/rhetoric
199 Chapter 24

Listening vs. Talking

Like many Chinese ideas and concepts, Guiguzi is based on the yin-yang approach, two opposites in perfect harmony. Listening and talking. Not just talking because we want to say something, but talking based on what was said, how it was said, and why it was said. In a more general sense, managing a situation in response to circumstances. Guiguzi uses the open-shut terminology referring to our mouths. The open-shut are intertwined and correlated, interacting with each other to adapt and respond to the constantly changing situation. There are actions and inactions: flexible, adjustable, and responsive.

Although people differ naturally, each with their own personality and story, topics are infinite and changes are endless; a speaker who uses the open-shut technique can build a solid foundation for negotiation, see all solutions, and control the conversation and its outcome. As such, quoted in Chapter 24 mentioned above, "It is by adapting myself to his disposition that I can manage him. I follow him to understand him, to lead him."

This technique is not only for persuasion, but to connect with people and make allies and spies more easily. By adapting to the will of others, trust is earned, connections are made, and influence can occur. But to adapt, we must listen. Listen to learn, not only about them but about how to speak next about their reality and point of view. It is important, therefore, to not overpower the audience by "trying to convince" with speech. Refer to the Pooh chapter. Leave space. Listen.

Paradoxically, listening is more important in persuasion than talking. It is critical to understand and to use this understanding to create a relationship. It is only then that efficient persuasion can occur. As such, listening is not a passive act, it is an active engagement of both you, the listener, and the speakers. Do not force upon others what they do not want; do not teach them what they do not wish to know. Learn about what they like and dislike and speak accordingly.

The Other vs. the Self

Another paradox in efficient rhetoric is that listening to the other is useless unless you listen to yourself. In other words, how can you influence or persuade another to go in a certain direction if you do not know what direction you want them to go? To know this direction, you must know your own finality, destination, and how this person can help you along the way. To know yourself means to know where you are, and where you are headed. By listening and examining the other, the efficient manager continuously reflects upon himself to see if the gained knowledge changes his perspective. But again, to know if there are subtle changes, you must know what there is initially. Understanding others starts from the understanding of the self. Never take for granted that "you know" before the conversation evolves because the conversation should make your knowledge change, evolve, and adapt. At the end of a conversation, you should ask yourself: How did I grow?

Regardless of the topic or the new knowledge, try to remain calm; a calm mind sees more clearly and is not clouded by emotions. Stress, anxiety, frustration, or impatience do not serve to open up or serve the real analysis of what is said, and this faulty analysis leads to faulty actions. As said in the Guiguzi, "A lack of self-discipline leads to mismanagement of others."[200]

Smooth vs. Cracked

Look at the strongest rock in detail as that is the only way to reveal small cracks. Once the cracks are revealed, then they can be exploited. The same is true of the words of others. The more you inspect, the more you can find an illogical argument or point, a contradiction, a gesture or fleeting gaze, something that is not as solid as it seems to one who is not paying attention (external signs will often reveal internal feelings, don't listen with your ears only). The door is open, and with the open-shut strategy, the crack will expose a way in, not necessarily a way to challenge, but a way into their confidence, their trust, a way to make them open up. Mending the crack will create alliances, trying to widen the crack will create resistance. The

---

200 Chapter 2

efficient manager obviously needs more alliances and less resistance.

Stability vs. Fluidity

Do not insist. As long as your open-shut strategy provides new information and new ways to direct the conversation, follow them. However, when the other party does not speak or what they say does not contain sufficient information to steer the conversation, insisting may only provoke their defenses and further shutdown. In that case, it may be best to change the direction of the discussion, continue to establish trust, and follow a different thread that may lead you to where you need to go via a different path. Again, do not assume you know. Follow the flow of the conversation and the knowledge acquisition. Pivot if required.

Adjust yourself according to circumstances, and others will know nothing of your actions.

Putting It All Together

These are a few of the highlights of the Guiguzi that the efficient manager can readily apply. Without seeing any benefits for himself, a skeptical person will not change his mind, so listening is the key to learning what benefits could be of value. The less you struggle to align others to your finality, the more allies and spies you will have, and the more your progress will be fast, continuous, and effortless, I could even say traceless.

CHAPTER 50

MANAGING MEETINGS

"ALL WARFARE IS based on deception."[201] This is one of the most well-known quotes from Sun Tzu's *The Art of War*. He continues with this example, "Hence, when able to attack, we must seem unable; when using our forces, we must seem inactive; when we are near, we must make the enemy believe we are far away; when far away, we must make him believe we are near."[202]

This means being unpredictable, destabilizing the opponent, never using the same tactic twice since it will not be a surprise and the conditions for success will be different.

Now let's apply this to the efficient manager's life.

Before Meetings

People come into meetings with expectations of what will happen. They carry over their mood and their experiences from previous meetings. They come with desired outcomes based on who they are.[203]

---

201 Translation from Lionel Giles, Chapter I, line 18
202 Translation from Lionel Giles, Chapter I, line 19
203 See the story of the baker, Chapter 35

If they come in stressed, they will behave in a stressed-out manner. They may be more anxious, impatient, condescending, or on the defensive. If they come in with this state of mind, they will not contribute positively and be there to build a solution, which is obviously not a great place to be for an efficient manager.

If possible, try to find out as much as you can about the main stakeholders of the meeting, the people of influence beforehand. How is their mood today? What is their state of mind coming into the meeting? A quick discussion before or at the start of the meeting will allow you to capture these details. Knowing their state of mind will allow the efficient manager to do two things:

- **Calibrate accordingly** Every golfer chooses their club according to distance, winds, and terrain. They adjust according to situations. Do not say what you want or need; adjust according to the mood of the audience or to the most important members of the audience.
- **Change the mood** A lot of public speakers will start by making a joke to relax the crowd and make them more receptive. I'm not saying to make a joke to make people laugh, but by changing the mood, you control the mood you are setting.

These serve to influence the ambiance and the state of mind before the meeting starts, makes people more open to what you will say, and creates positive, constructive energy. As quoted above, all warfare is based on deception.

As I said in Managing Delegation,[204] if you control the environment, you control how people grow. It is the same for meetings. If you control the environment, the rest will occur naturally. Once the seed has been put in the ground by situations and circumstances, then everything to make it grow properly is but a reaction to the fact it was planted. As the Dutch inspirational speaker Alexander Den Heijer said, "When a flower doesn't bloom, you fix the environment in which it grows, not the flower."[205]

The earlier you act on a tendency, the less you act on it. Our need for efficiency decreases with the deployment of the initial tendency; the more the real is concretely determined, the more it takes power, energy, heroism, to alter it. Acting beforehand creates an effect in the distance instead of a direct head-on.

Control the mood, then control the patterns, and control the conversation.

During Meetings

The same holds true midway in meetings, of course, but a particularly good example is when the conversation is either not going in the direction you want or is stagnant and not progressing (we all have experienced stagnant brainstorm sessions, for example).

In cases like this, just trying to bring a new topic may work or not. What does work is completely breaking the

204 Chapter 47
205 Goodreads.com, Alexander Den Heijer Quotes

pattern by saying or doing something totally unexpected to completely break the established pattern and not slowly steer it, but surprisingly change it. This pivot takes people by surprise, so much so that it opens up the suggestion of rebasing the conversation.

Therefore, change the mood to control the mood and, eventually, the conversation.

We have discussed how the efficient manager strives in chaos.[206] This pivoting approach creates unexpected chaos — unexpected for all others, but totally under control from your perspective, which is manageable and optimizable.

Know and Guide

Instead of pretending to manage the meeting by directly attacking the situation and trying to make a heroic maneuver, the wise manager knows that they must go through a transforming process to imply and achieve the effect.

You must detect in advance the conditions of possibility (or create/change them if these initial conditions do not point in the proper direction) and guide the evolution of the situation or the meeting in the desired direction. You are only continuously improving the situation based on the effects implied within this situation and its potential. In other words, by always following and being carried by the flow, you have access to a much richer position of all possible effects compared to the one working hard to lead.

---

206 Chapter 38

CHAPTER 51

MANAGING THE OTHER ORG CHART

PREVIOUSLY I DISCUSSED THE traditional org chart[207] and its pitfalls to uncover who supports who and what layer really brings value and importance. This traditional org chart is one of hierarchy only.

But in any company, hierarchy is only what is "supposed" to be. There are games of power, influence, and politics. There are friendships and debts to be paid. There are allies, spies, foes, and threats.

Now, this is a much more interesting org chart and an important one to understand for the efficient manager.

From the Efficient Manager's Perspective

I've mentioned before that the role of the efficient manager is to achieve their finality with the least effort and energy possible.[208] I've defined what allies and spies are.[209] I've defined direct and indirect influences.[210] You've seen how

207 Chapter 44
208 Chapters 1 and 22
209 Chapter 14
210 Chapter 39

to coach[211] or make someone progress based on where they want to go and where you think they need to go.

Now is the time to put it all together.

The technique, while simple to illustrate once you know all that needs to be known, is actually hard to build. Start by building the real org chart of all the levels and departments that have a say, an influence in either helping you or preventing you from achieve your finality. This means your direct north and south lines of command, your direct peer colleagues, but it can also mean other departments such as customer support, production, product definition, and so on if you are in sales.

Above each department, make sure to write down why and how this department impacts your finality. Then try to figure out what the finality of that department is and who is its head.

The next step, with a different colored pen, is to draw lines describing your particular relationship with everyone. If you do not have a relationship with a certain person, draw no lines for now. Use a red line for a foe or a threat (someone who could prevent you from achieving or who doesn't like you, etc.) and a green line for friends and allies. Use a blue line for spies and create your own colour code. These lines do not necessarily respect hierarchy lines, of course. The janitor can be a personal friend and a spy, whereas the VP of a different department may resent you from a previous life.

---

211 Chapter 18

Now you have a pretty good idea of where and how you stand, whom you can count on, and who you should leverage or avoid, etc.

From the Network's Perspective

To know yourself is not sufficient. You need to know the entire picture, or as Sun Tzu puts it, to know your enemy: "If you know the enemy and know yourself, you need not fear the result of a hundred battles. If you know yourself but not the enemy, for every victory gained you will also suffer a defeat."[212]

Go back to that org chart you just did, and with different colors, or textures (dashed lines for example) add all that you know. Who is a friend of whom, who is a threat or a foe to whom? Do those two VPs work well together or do they hate each other? Is that director from department A able to easily influence my boss and, if so, why? Do people in my team have direct access as close allies to levels above my head?

Map all you know. Put question marks in all that you don't know but that knowing would be critical (these are mainly from threats and foes from people who can directly influence your success. For example, does this threat have a personal relationship with this person whom I really need help from …?) You end up with something like this:

---

212 Translation from Lionel Giles, Chapter III, line 18

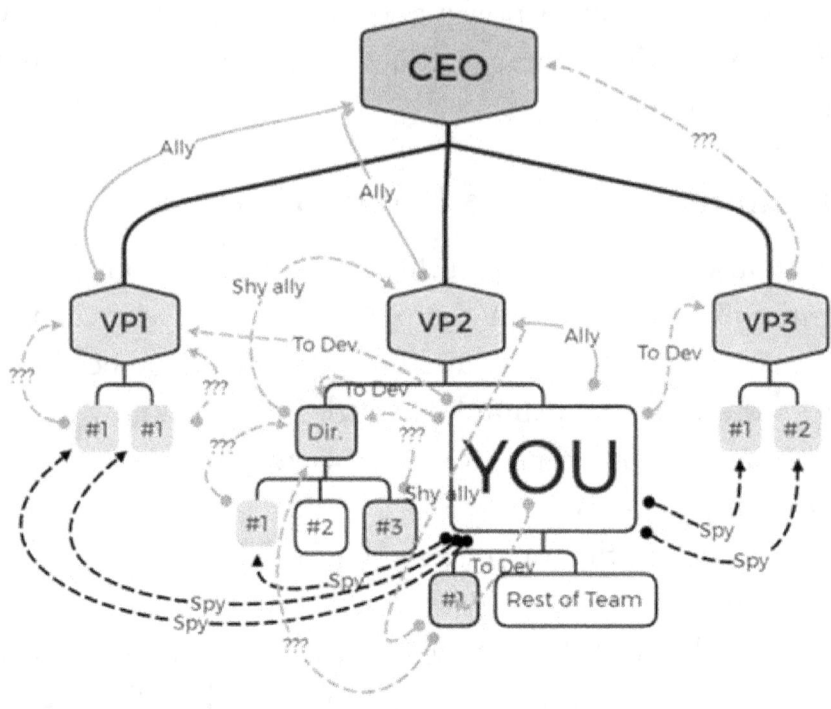

Figure 17: Strategic and influence org chart

Then the Fun Part

The fun part starts here. The real managerial work. The efficient manager's magic.

For each key individual on that chart, an ally, a spy, a friend, foe, or threat, create a table: What do you need to happen, to avoid, from that person? What relationship do you need to build? What information in your chart is missing that you need to know?

And for each line, make a strategy.

For example, this individual is potentially a threat because they do not believe you have the capabilities to do the job or do not believe in your vision or the usefulness of your team. Now that you know that:

- Should you try to change this person's perspective? If so, how? Directly or indirectly? By professional means (business justification) or by becoming a friend? Or by making them "see" that the presence of your group, on a personal level, helps them shine?
- You believe this person is a personal friend of my boss' boss. What is your strategy to find that out because if your belief is true, it could mean trouble for you.
- If it's true and if you cannot befriend them, how can you make sure, for example, to discredit their opinion of your group toward deciders without discrediting them since you don't want to have the professional threat become a personal one.
- And so on ...

As mentioned above, for each line, build a strategy. For each question mark, build a strategy. As you do this, maybe person A will end up in four different strategies, so how can you cope with that? Are they complimentary or opposite? Can you kill two birds with a single stone?

How do you deploy all those strategies while still doing your job? Isn't improving the position of your team to achieve finality the very definition of your job? Don't get lost in too many operational tasks and start to manage and shape the environment according to the achievement of that finality.

As I said before, every single interaction and opportunity is a chance to manage. Don't waste too many.

CHAPTER 52

MANAGING
THE ZEN MANAGER

TO BECOME AN EFFICIENT manager, there are 51 previous chapters filled with tips and approaches. All these can lead to effortless and successful management with less pressure, less stress, and less anxiety, but more results and achievements. Reduced stress and anxiety are paths to becoming not only an efficient manager, but also a Zen efficient manager.

We have discussed how to create habits in others[213] and how to avoid procrastination in others.[214] These are all true for us as well. We discussed how to shape the environment to have predictable, effortless outcomes.[215] We discussed self-mastery[216] and hindrances[217] that can mine our own path to this self-mastery. We also highlighted the importance, in rhetoric, to know your path and your destination.[218]

---

213 Chapter 37
214 Chapter 45
215 Chapter 17
216 Chapter 10
217 Chapter 27
218 Chapter 49

We concluded the chapter on Managing Delegation[219] with this sentence, referring to how we could make people do things without asking them to actually do those things: "Try to shape water...The only way you will ever succeed is by shaping its environment. As it turns out, what is true for others is also true for you."

In other words, shape your own environment in a way that makes you become what you want to become.

Eckhart Tolle once said, "Stress is caused by being here, yet wanting to be there."[220] How can you be here, but make sure that time brings you there...?

Shaping the Environment

You would like to have a more peaceful life, yet you always put on loud music...You would like to stop eating sugar, yet your pantry is full of cookies...You would like to be more focused, yet your desk is a mess.

We discussed coherence[221] to teach, coach, and make others progress. The concept applies to you as well. What you do today, what you think, why, how, where, what, and whom you surround yourself with will create the future you. When faced with a fork in the road, imagine yourself at the end of your life looking back at the choices you are now facing. From that vantage point, what do you wish you had chosen at this juncture?

---

219 Chapter 47
220 Goodreads.com, Eckhart Tolle Quotes
221 Chapter 41

A big hindrance in becoming who you would like to become is coherence. You would like to grow a mango tree, yet you live in a Nordic climate…This will obviously fail. Then why create patterns as a manager that do not naturally guide you in the direction you want to go?

The simple answers to those questions are, of course:

- Because we don't know where we are currently
- Because we don't know where we want to go
- Because we don't take the time to think about those two questions

As such, we do what we know how to do, and we shape our environment to help us do it instead of shaping our environment to help us become what we want to become. To quote Master Oogway from *Kung Fu Panda*, "When the path you walk always leads back to yourself, you never get anywhere …"[222]

When you are in the operational domain, you focus on the consequences. When you migrate to the managerial domain, your focus centers on the causes. And then you realize why you are still where you were, as a manager, even if the responsibilities or the titles have changed.

Look At Your Nails

Have you ever noticed how your nails can be awesome teachers? In this age of instant gratification, with everything

222 https://www.quotes.net/mquote/1029547

always at our fingertips, we sometimes forget that true change takes time.

Watch your nails for a few seconds. Did you see them grow? Of course not, but chances are, a few weeks from now they will have grown, but you will have more than likely trimmed them.

As Aristotle said, "As it is not one swallow or a fine day that makes a spring, so it is not one day or a short time that makes a man blessed and happy."[223]

Changes take time and patience. They take a plan, a vision, and they require a knowledge of where you are and where you want to go. Once you have this, ask yourself, what is the next single action I can do to move in that direction? And what can change around me to help me in that quest and help me create those new habits?

Slowly new habits will take place, including the habit of being efficient and Zen. We are good at what we practice, as discussed in the chapter on managing expertise.[224]

By slowly transforming, we create a habit of being Zen and efficient.

In other words, to become a Zen efficient manager, the most important work you need to do is not to coach others, to train others, to manage meetings or to manage time, it is to know yourself and shape the environment to guide you to transform. When you know yourself and shape the environment accordingly, you can bridge that gap (as seen

223 Goodreads.com, Aristotle Quotes
224 Chapter 19

in Chapter 42) between what you do and who you are. When you start at an unknown "somewhere" and head to a different unknown "somewhere," you'll end up nowhere.

Mastery and Humility

To become the master of time, you must stop being dependent on it. To become the master of your agenda, stop depending on it. To become a master of your smartphone, guess what? Stop being dependent on it.

The same holds true for management and for life. To become the master of them, you must let go of being dependent on habits and bad habits based on the thought that "this is who I am." To help remove those habits, shape your environment so the habits become irrelevant, only nuisances. It is hard to put extra water in a full glass, whereas the empty one is full of potential. By letting go of old habits, you create room for the something you want to progress toward. As such, I would argue that the most important quality that an efficient and Zen manager needs to cultivate is humility. Only then can you create room to listen, learn, empower, coach, transform, and become.

In closing, a last quote from Lao Tzu: "He who controls others may be powerful, but he who has mastered himself is mightier still."[225]

---

225 Goodreads.com, Lao Tzu Quotes

LIST OF FIGURES

LIST OF TABLES

www.ingramcontent.com/pod-product-compliance
Lightning Source LLC
Chambersburg PA
CBHW061137120626
46546CB00005B/1828